The History of Richard the Second

The History of Richard the Second

Makers of History Series (Annotated)

Jacob Abbott

Cedar Lake Classics

Copyright © 2023 by Cedar Lake Classics

This is an annotated edition of a public domain work.

CONTENTS

PREFACE vii
PHOTO INSERT viii

1 | Richard's Predecessors 1

2 | Quarrels 16

3 | The Black Prince 38

4 | The Battle of Poictiers 51

5 | Childhood of Richard 72

6 | Accession to the Throne 88

7 | The Coronation 99

8 | Chivalry 107

9 | Wat Tyler's Insurrection 124

10 | The End of the Insurrection 141

11 | Good Queen Anne 153

12 | Incidents of the Reign 165

CONTENTS

13 | The Little Queen 178

14 | Richard's Deposition and Death 187

ABOUT JACOB ABBOTT 201
BIOGRAPHIES ABBOTT WROTE 203

PREFACE

King Richard the Second lived in the days when the chivalry of feudal times was in all its glory. His father, the Black Prince; his uncles, the sons of Edward the Third, and his ancestors in a long line, extending back to the days of Richard the First, were among the most illustrious knights of Europe in those days, and their history abounds in the wonderful exploits, the narrow escapes, and the romantic adventures, for which the knights errant of the Middle Ages were so renowned. This volume takes up the story of English history at the death of Richard the First, and continues it to the time of the deposition and death of Richard the Second, with a view of presenting as complete a picture as is possible, within such limits, of the ideas and principles, the manners and customs, and the extraordinary military undertakings and exploits of that wonderful age.

Parley with the Insurgents

1

Richard's Predecessors

Three Richards.—Richard the Crusader.—King John.—Character of the kings and nobles of those days.—Origin and nature of their power.—Natural rights of man in respect to the fruits of the earth.—Beneficial results of royal rule.—The power of kings and nobles was restricted.—Disputes about the right of succession.—Case of young Arthur.—The King of France becomes his ally.—Map showing the situation of Normandy.—Arthur is defeated and made prisoner.—John attempts to induce Arthur to abdicate.—Account of the assassination of Arthur.—Various accounts of the mode of Arthur's death.—Uncertainty in respect to these stories.—League formed against him by his barons.—Portrait of King John.—Magna Charta.—Runny Mead.—The agreement afterward repudiated.—New wars.—New ratifications of Magna Charta.—Cruelties and oppressions practiced upon the Jews.—Extract from the old chronicles.—Absurd accusations.—The story of the crucified child.—John Lexinton.—Confessions extorted by torture.—Injustice and cruelty of the practice.—Anecdotes of the nobles and the king.

THERE have been three monarchs of the name of Richard upon the English throne.

Richard I. is known and celebrated in history as Richard the Crusader. He was the sovereign ruler not only of England, but of all the Norman part of France, and from both of his dominions he raised a vast army, and went with it to the Holy Land, where he fought many years against the Saracens with a view of rescuing Jerusalem and the other holy places there from the dominion of unbelievers. He met with a great many remarkable adventures in going to the Holy Land, and with still more remarkable ones on his return home, all of which are fully related in the volume of this series entitled King Richard I.

Richard II. did not succeed Richard I. immediately. Several reigns intervened. The monarch who immediately succeeded Richard I. was John. John was Richard's brother, and had been left in command, in England, as regent, during the king's absence in the Holy Land.

After John came Henry III. and the three Edwards; and when the third Edward died, his son Richard II. was heir to the throne. He was, however, too young at that time to reign, for he was only ten years old.

The kings in these days were wild and turbulent men, always engaged in wars with each other and with their nobles, while all the industrial classes were greatly depressed. The nobles lived in strong castles in various places about the country, and owned, or claimed to own, very large estates, which the laboring men were compelled to cultivate for them. Some of these castles still remain in a habitable state, but most of them are now in ruins—and very curious objects the ruins are to see.

The kings held their kingdoms very much as the nobles did their estates—they considered them theirs by right. And the people generally thought so too. The king had a *right*, as they imagined, to live in luxury and splendor, and to lord it over the country, and compel the mass of the people to pay him nearly all their earnings in rent and taxes, and to raise armies, whenever he commanded them, to go and fight for him in his quarrels with his neighbors, because his father had done these things before him. And what right had his father to do these things? Why, because *his* father had done them before him. Very well; but to go back to the beginning. What right had the first man to assume this power, and how did he get possession of it? This was a question that nobody could answer, for nobody knew then, and nobody knows now, who were the original founders of these noble families, or by what means they first came into power. People did not know how to read and write in the days when kings first began to reign, and so no records ere made, and no accounts kept of public transactions; and when at length the countries of Europe in the Middle Ages began to emerge somewhat into the light of civilization, these royal and noble families were found every where established. The whole territory of Europe was divided into a great number of kingdoms, principalities, dukedoms, and other such sovereignties, over each of which some ancient family was established in supreme and almost despotic power. Nobody knew how they originally came by their power.

Ruins of an Ancient Castle

The people generally submitted to this power very willingly. In the first place, they had a sort of blind veneration for it on account of its ancient and established character. Then they were always taught from infancy that kings had a right to reign, and nobles a right to their estates, and that to toil all their lives, and allow their kings and nobles to take, in rent and taxes, and in other such ways, every thing that they, the people, earned, except what was barely sufficient for their subsistence, was an obligation which the God of nature had imposed upon them, and that it would be a sin in them not to submit to it; whereas nothing can be more plain than that the God of nature intends the *earth* for *man*, and that consequently society ought to be so organized that in each generation every man can enjoy something at least like his fair share of the products of it, in proportion to the degree of industry or skill which he brings to bear upon the work of developing these products.

There was another consideration which made the common people more inclined to submit to these hereditary kings and nobles than we should have supposed they would have been, and that is, the government which they exercised was really, in many respects, of great benefit to the community. They preserved order as far as they could, and punished crimes. If bands of robbers were formed, the nobles or the king sent out a troop to put them down. If a thief broke into a house and stole what he found there, the government sent officers to pursue and arrest him, and then shut him up in jail. If a murder was committed, they would seize the murderer and hang him. It was their interest to do this, for if they allowed the people to be robbed and plundered, or to live all the time in fear of violence, then it is plain that the cultivation of the earth could not go on, and the rents and the taxes could not be paid. So these governments established courts, and made laws, and appointed officers to execute them, in order to protect the lives and property of their subjects from all common thieves and murderers, and the people were taught to believe that there was no other way by which their protection could be secured except by the power of the kings. We must be contented as we are, they said to themselves, and be willing to go and fight the king's battles, and to pay to him and to the nobles nearly every thing that we can earn, or else society will be thrown into confusion, and the whole land will be full of thieves and murderers.

In the present age of the world, means have been devised by which, in any country sufficiently enlightened for this purpose, the people themselves can organize a government to restrain and punish robbers and murderers, and to make and execute all other necessary laws for the promotion of the general welfare; but in those ancient times this was seldom or never done. The art of government was not then understood. It is very imperfectly understood at the present day, but in those days it was not understood at all; and, accordingly, there was nothing better for the people to do than to submit to, and not only to submit to, but to maintain with all their power the government of these hereditary kings and nobles.

It must not be supposed, however, that the power of these hereditary nobles was absolute. It was very far from being absolute. It was restricted and curtailed by the ancient customs and laws of the realm, which customs and laws the kings and nobles could not transgress without producing insurrections and rebellions. Their own right to the power which they wielded rested solely on ancient customs, and, of course, the restrictions on these rights, which had come down by custom from ancient times, were as valid as the rights themselves.

Notwithstanding this, the kings were continually overstepping the limits of their power, and insurrections and civil wars were all the time breaking out, in consequence of which the realms over which they reigned were kept in a perpetual state of turmoil. These wars arose sometimes from the contests of different claimants to the crown. If a king died, leaving only a son too young to rule, one of his brothers, perhaps—an uncle of the young prince—would attempt to seize the throne, under one pretext or another, and then the nobles and the courtiers would take sides, some in favor of the nephew and some in favor of the uncle, and a long civil war would perhaps ensue. This was the case immediately after the death of Richard I. When he died he designated as his successor a nephew of his, who was at that time only twelve years old. The name of this young prince was Arthur. He was the son of Geoffrey, a brother of Richard's, older than John, and he was accordingly the rightful heir; but John, having been once installed in power by his brother—for his brother had made him regent when he went away on his crusade to the Holy Land—determined that he would seize the crown himself, and exclude his nephew from the succession.

So he caused himself to be proclaimed king. He was in Normandy at the time; but he immediately put himself at the head of an armed force and went to England.

The barons of the kingdom immediately resolved to resist him, and to maintain the cause of the young Arthur. They said that Arthur was the rightful king, and that John was only a usurper; so they withdrew, every man to his castle, and fortified themselves there.

In cases like this, where in any kingdom there were two contested claims for the throne, the kings of the neighboring countries usually came in and took part in the quarrel. They thought that by taking sides with one of the claimants, and aiding him to get possession of the throne, they should gain an influence in the kingdom which they might afterward turn to account for themselves. The King of France at this time was named Philip. He determined to espouse the cause of young Arthur in this quarrel. His motive for doing this was to have a pretext for making war upon John, and, in the war, of conquering some portion of Normandy and annexing it to his own dominions.

So he invited Arthur to come to his court, and when he arrived there he asked him if he would not like to be King of England. Arthur said that he should like to be a king very much indeed. "Well," said Philip, "I will furnish you with an army, and you shall go and make war upon John. I will go too, with another army; then, whatever I shall take away from John in Normandy shall be mine, but all of England shall be yours."

The situation of the country of Normandy, in relation to France and to England, may be seen by the accompanying map.

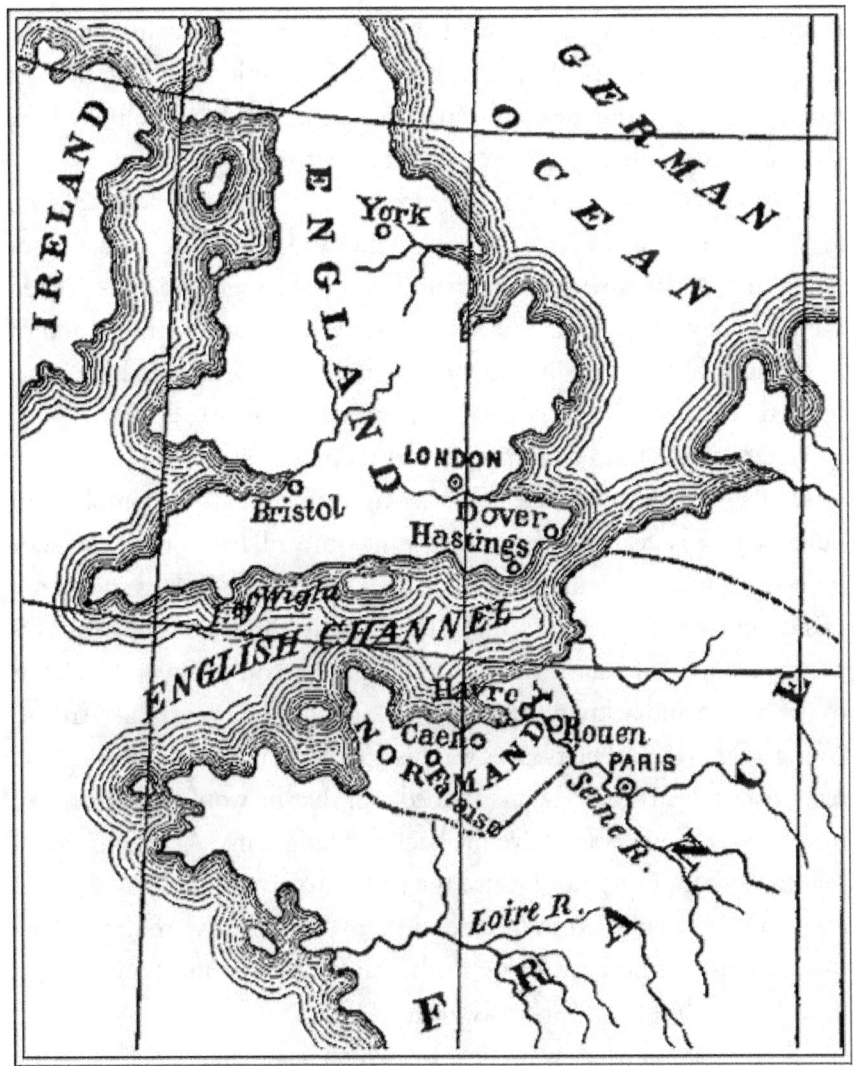

Map: Situation of Normandy

Philip thought that he could easily seize a large part of Normandy and annex it to his dominions while John was engaged in defending himself against Arthur in England.

Arthur, who was at this time only about fourteen years old, was, of course, too young to exercise any judgment in respect to such questions as these, so he readily agreed to what Philip proposed, and very soon afterward Philip assembled an army, and, placing Arthur nominally at the head of it, he sent him forth into Normandy to commence the war upon John. Of course, Arthur was only nominally at the head of the army. There were old and experienced generals who really had the command, though they did every thing in Arthur's name.

A long war ensued, but in the end Arthur's army was defeated, and Arthur himself was made prisoner. John and his savage soldiery got possession of the town where Arthur was in the night, and they seized the poor boy in his bed. The soldiers took him away with a troop of horse, and shut him up in a dungeon in a famous castle called the castle of Falaise. You will see the position of Falaise on the map.

After a while John determined to visit Arthur in his prison, in order to see if he could not make some terms with him. To accomplish his purpose more effectually, he waited some time, till he thought the poor boy's spirit must be broken down by his confinement and his sufferings. His design was probably to make terms with him by offering him his liberty, and perhaps some rich estate, if he would only give up his claims to the crown and acknowledge John as king; but he found that Arthur, young as he was, and helpless as was his condition in his lonely dungeon, remained in heart entirely unsubdued. All that he would say in answer to John's proposal was, "Give me back my kingdom." At length, John, finding that he could not induce the prince to give up his claims, went away in a rage, and determined to kill him. If Arthur were dead, there would then, he thought, be no farther difficulty, for all acknowledged that after Arthur he himself was the next heir.

There was another way, too, by which John might become the rightful heir to the crown. It was a prevalent idea in those days that no person who was blind, or deaf, or dumb could inherit a crown. To blind young Arthur, then, would be as effectual a means of extinguishing his claims as to kill him, and John accordingly determined to destroy the young prince's right to the succession by putting out his eyes; so he sent two executioners to perform this cruel deed upon the captive in his dungeon.

The name of the governor of the castle was Hubert. He was a kind and humane man, and he pitied his unhappy prisoner; and so, when the executioners came, and Hubert went to the cell to tell Arthur that they had come, and what they had come for, Arthur fell on his knees before him and began to beg for mercy, crying out, Save me! oh, save me! with such piteous cries that Hubert's heart was moved with compassion, and he concluded that he would put off the execution of the dreadful deed till he could see the king again.

John was very angry when he found that his orders had not been obeyed, and he immediately determined to send Arthur to another prison, which was in the town of Rouen, the keeper of which he knew to be an unscrupulous and merciless man. This was done, and soon afterward it was given out through all the kingdom that Arthur was dead. Every body was convinced that John had caused him to be murdered. There were several different rumors in respect to the way in which the deed was done. One story was that John, being at Rouen, where Arthur was imprisoned, after having become excited with the wine which he had drunk at a carousal, went and killed Arthur himself with his own hand, and that he then ordered his body to be thrown into the Seine, with heavy stones tied to the feet to make it sink. The body, however, afterward, they said, rose to the surface and floated to the shore, where some monks found it, and buried it secretly in their abbey.

Another story was that John pretended to be reconciled to Arthur, and took him out one day to ride with him, with other horsemen. Presently John rode on with Arthur in advance of the party, until late in the evening they came to a solitary place where there was a high cliff overhanging the sea. Here John drew his sword, and, riding up to Arthur, suddenly ran him through the body. Arthur cried aloud, and begged for mercy as he fell from his horse to the ground; but John dragged him to the edge of the precipice, and threw him over into the sea while he was yet alive and breathing.

A third story was that John had determined that Arthur must die, and that he came himself one night to the castle where Arthur was confined in Rouen on the Seine. A man went up to Arthur's room, and, waking him from his sleep, directed him to rise.

"Rise," said he, "and come with me."

Arthur rose, and followed his guard with fear and trembling. They descended the staircase to the foot of the tower, where there was a portal that opened close upon the river. On going out, Arthur found that there was a boat there at the stairs, with his uncle and some other men in it. Arthur at once understood what these things meant, and was greatly terrified. He fell on his knees, and begged his uncle to spare his life; but John gave a sign, and Arthur was stabbed, and then taken out a little way and thrown into the river. Some say that John killed him and threw him into the river with his own hand.

Which of these tales is true, if either of them is so, can now probably never be known. All that is certain is that John in some way or other caused Arthur to be murdered in order to remove him out of the way. He justified his claim to the crown by pretending that King Richard, his brother, on his deathbed, bequeathed the kingdom to him, but this nobody believes.

At any rate, John obtained possession of the crown, and he reigned many years. His reign, however, was a very troubled one. His title, indeed, after Arthur's death, was no longer disputed, but he was greatly abhorred and hated for his cruelties and crimes, and at length nearly all the barons of his realm banded themselves together against him, with the view of reducing his power as king within more reasonable bounds.

The king fought these *rebels*, as he called them, for some time, but he was continually beaten, and finally compelled to yield to them. They wrote out their demands in a full and formal manner upon parchment, and compelled the king to sign it. This document was called the MAGNA CHARTA, which means the great charter.

The signing and delivering this deed is considered one of the most important events in English history. It was the first great covenant that was made between the kings and the people of England, and the stipulations of it have been considered binding to this day, so that it is, in some sense, the original basis and foundation of the civil rights which the British people now enjoy.

The place of assembly where King John came out to sign this covenant was a broad and beautiful meadow on the banks of the Thames, not far from Windsor Castle. The name of the field is Runny Mead. The word *mead* is a contraction for meadow.

King John

The act of once signing such a compact as this was, however, not sufficient, it seems, to bind the English kings. There were a great many disputes and contests about it afterward between the kings and the barons, as the kings, one after another, refused to adhere to the agreement made by John in their name, on the ground, perhaps, of the deed not being a voluntary one on his part. He was forced to sign it, they said, because the barons were stronger than he was. Of course, when the kings thought that they, in their turn, were stronger than the barons, they were very apt to violate the agreement. One of the kings on one occasion obtained a dispensation from the Pope, absolving him from all obligation to fulfill this compact.

In consequence of this want of good faith on the part of the kings, there arose continually new quarrels, and sometimes new civil wars, between the kings and the barons. In these contests the barons were usually successful in the end, and then they always insisted on the vanquished monarch's ratifying or signing the Magna Charta anew. It is said that in this way it was confirmed and re-established not less than *thirty times* in the course of four or five reigns, and thus it became at last the settled and unquestioned law of the land. The power of the kings of England has been restricted and controlled by its provisions ever since.

All this took place in the reigns preceding the accession of Richard II.

Besides these contests with the barons, the kings of those times were often engaged in contentions with the people; but the people, having no means of combining together or otherwise organizing their resistance, were almost always compelled to submit. They were often oppressed and maltreated in the most cruel manner. The great object of the government seems to have been to extort money from them in every possible way, and to this end taxes and imposts were levied upon them to such an extent as to leave them enough only for bare subsistence. The most cruel means were often resorted to to compel the payment of these taxes. The unhappy Jews were the special subjects of these extortions. The Jews in Europe were at this time generally excluded from almost every kind of business except buying and selling movable property, and lending money; but by these means many of them became very rich, and their property was of such a nature that it could be easily concealed. This led to a great many cases of cruelty in the treatment of them by the government. The government pretended often that they were richer than they really were, while they themselves pretended that they were poorer than they were, and the government resorted to the most lawless and atrocious measures sometimes to compel them to pay. The following extract from one of the historians of the time gives an example of this cruelty, and, at the same time, furnishes the reader with a specimen of the quaint and curious style of composition and orthography in which the chronicles of those days are written.

[Furthermore, about the same time, the King taxed the Jewes, and greeuouslie tormented and emprisoned them bicause divers of them would not willinglie pay the summes that they were taxed at. Amongst other, there was one of them at Bristow who would not consent to give any fine for his deliverance; wherefore by the king's commandment he was put unto this penance, namely, that eurie daie, till he would agree to give to the king those ten thousand marks that he was siezed at, he would have one of his teeth plucked out of his head. By the space of seaun daies together he stood stedfast, losing euerie of those days a tooth. But on the eighth day, when he shuld come to have the eighth tooth, and the last (for he had but eight in all), draun out, he paid the monie to save that, who with more wisedome and less paine might have done so before, and so have saved his seven teeth which he lost with such torments; for those homelie toothdrauers used no great cunning in plucking them forth, as may be conjectured.]

The poor Jews were entirely at the mercy of the king in these cases, for they were so much hated and despised by the Christian people of the land that nobody was disposed to defend them, either by word or deed, whatever injustice or cruelty they might suffer. The most absurd and injurious charges were made against them by common rumor, and were generally believed, for there was nobody to defend them. There was a story, for example, that they were accustomed every year to crucify a Christian child. One year a mother, having missed her child, searched every where for him, and at length found him dead in the bottom of a well. It was recollected that a short time before the child disappeared he had been seen playing with some Jewish children before the door of a house where a certain Jew lived, called John Lexinton. The story was immediately circulated that this child had been taken by the Jews and crucified. It was supposed, of course, that John Lexinton was intimately connected with the crime. He was immediately seized by the officers, and he was so terrified by their threats and denunciations that he promised to confess everything if they would spare his life. This they engaged to do, and he accordingly made what he called his confession.

In consequence of this confession a hundred and two Jews were apprehended, and carried to London and shut up in the Tower.

But, notwithstanding the confession that John Lexinton had made and the promise that was given him, it was determined that he should not be spared, but should die. Upon hearing this he was greatly distressed, and he offered to make more confessions; so he revealed several additional particulars in regard to the crime, and implicated numerous other persons in the commission of it. All was, however, of no avail. He was executed, and eighteen other Jews with him.

Judging from the evidence which we have in this case, it is highly probable that the alleged crime was wholly imaginary. Confessions that are extorted by pain or fear are never to be believed. They may be true, but they are far more likely to be false. It was the custom in ancient times, and it still remains the custom among many ignorant and barbarous nations, to put persons to torture in order to compel them to confess crimes of which they are suspected, or to reveal the names of their accomplices, but nothing can be more cruel or unjust than such a practice as this. Most men, in such cases, are so maddened with their agony and terror that they will say anything whatever that they think will induce their tormentors to put an end to their sufferings.

The common people could not often resist the acts of oppression which they suffered from their rulers, for they had no power, and they could not combine together extensively enough to create a power, and so they were easily kept in subjection.

The nobles, however, were much less afraid of the monarchs, and often resisted them and bid them defiance. It was the law in those days that all estates to which no other person had a legal claim *escheated*, as they called it, to the king. Of course, if the king could find an estate in which there was any flaw in the title of the man who held it, he would claim it for his own. At one time a king asked a certain baron to show him the title to his estate. He was intending to examine it, to see if there was any flaw in it. The baron, instead of producing his parchment, drew his sword and held it out before the king.

"This is my title to my estate," said he. "Your majesty will remember that William of Normandy did not conquer this realm for himself alone."

At another time a king wished to send two of his earls out of the country on some military expedition where they did not wish to go. They accordingly declined the undertaking.

"By the Almighty," said the king, "you shall either go or hang."

"By the Almighty," replied one of the earls, "we will neither go nor hang."

The nobles also often formed extensive and powerful combinations among each other against the king, and in such cases they were almost always successful in bringing him to submit to their demands.

2

Quarrels

A.D. 1327

Classes of quarrels in which the kings and the people were engaged.—The Pope.—His claim of jurisdiction in England.—The Pope's legate and the students at Oxford.—Great riot made by the students.—The end of the affair.—Plan to assassinate the king.—Margaret, the servant-girl.—Execution of Marish.—Ideas of the sacredness of the person of a king.—Origin of the wars with Leolin, Prince of Wales.—Leolin's bride interrupted at sea.—The unhappy fate of Leolin.—Fate of Prince David, his brother.—Occasional acts of generosity.—Story of Lewin and the box of dispatches.—The fate of Lewin.—Origin of the modern title of Prince of Wales.—The first English Prince of Wales.—Piers Gaveston.—Edward II. and his favorite.—Their wild and reckless behavior.—The king goes away to be married.—Edward's indifference on the occasion of his marriage.—His infatuation in respect to Gaveston.—The coronation.—Bold and presumptuous demeanor of Gaveston.—His unpopularity.—He is banished.—His parting.—The Black Dog of Ardenne.—Gaveston's return.—Gaveston made prisoner.—Consultation respecting him.—His fate.—The Spencers.—The queen and Mortimer.—Edward III. proclaimed king.—Edward II. made prisoner.—Edward II. formally deposed at Kenilworth.—The delegation require the king to abdicate the crown.—Opinion of the monks.—Alarm of the nobles.—Berkeley Castle.—Plot for assassinating the king.—Dreadful death.—Great hatred of Mortimer.—Situation of the castle of Nottingham.—The caves.—Entrance of the conspirators into the castle.—Isabella's unhappy fate.—Mortimer's Hole.

IN the days of the predecessors of King Richard the Second, notwithstanding the claim made by the kings of a right on their part to reign on account of the influence exercised by their government in promoting law and order throughout the community, the country was really kept in a continual state of turmoil by the quarrels which the different parties concerned in this government were engaged in with each other and with surrounding nations. These quarrels were of various kinds.

1. The kings, as we have already seen, were perpetually quarreling with the nobles.

2. The different branches of the royal family were often engaged in bitter and cruel wars with each other, arising from their conflicting claims to the crown.

3. The kings of different countries were continually making forays into each other's territories, or waging war against each other with fire and sword. These wars arose sometimes from a lawless spirit of depredation, and sometimes were waged to resent personal insults or injuries, real or imaginary.

4. The Pope of Rome, who claimed jurisdiction over the Church in England as well as elsewhere, was constantly coming into collision with the civil power.

From someone or other of these several causes, the kingdom of England, in the time of Richard's predecessors, was seldom at peace. Some great quarrel or other was continually going on. There was a great deal of difficulty during the reigns that immediately preceded that of Richard the Second between the kings and the Pope. The Pope, as has already been remarked, was considered the head of the whole Christian Church, and he claimed rights in respect to the appointment of the archbishops, and bishops, and other ecclesiastics in England, and in respect to the government and control of the monasteries, and the abbeys, and to the appropriation and expenditure of the revenues of the Church, which sometimes interfered very seriously with the views and designs of the king. Hence there arose continual disputes and quarrels. The Pope never came himself to England, but he often sent a grand embassador, called a legate, who traveled with great pomp and parade, and with many attendants, and assumed in all his doings a most lofty and superior air. In the contests in which these legates were engaged with the kings, the legates almost always came off conquerors through the immense influence which the Pope exercised over the consciences and religious fears of the mass of the people.

Sometimes the visits of the legates and their proceedings among the people led to open broils. At one time, for instance, the legate was at Oxford, where the great University, now so renowned throughout the world, already existed. He was lodged at an abbey there, and some of the scholars of the University wishing to pay their respects to him, as they said, went in a body to the gates of the abbey and demanded admission; but the porter kept them back and refused to let them in. Upon this a great noise and tumult arose, the students pressing against the gates to get in, and the porter, assisted by the legate's men, whom he called to his assistance, resisting them.

In the course of the fray one or two of the students succeeded in forcing their way in as far as to the kitchen of the abbey, and there one of them called upon a cook to help them. But the cook, instead of helping them, dipped out a ladle full of hot broth from a kettle and threw it into the student's face. Whereupon the other students cried out, as the ancient chronicler relates it, "What meane we to suffer this villanie," and, taking an arrow, he set it in his bow, having caught up these weapons in the beginning of the fray, and let it fly at the cook, and killed him on the spot.

This, of course, greatly increased the excitement. More students came in, and so great was the tumult and confusion that the legate was in terror for his life, and he fled and concealed himself in the belfry of the abbey. After lying in this place of concealment for some time, until the tumult was in some measure appeased, he crept out secretly, fled across the Thames, and then, mounting a horse, made the best of his way to London.

He made complaint to the king of the indignity which he had endured, and the king immediately sent a troop of armed men, with an earl at the head of them, to rescue the remainder of the legate's men that were still imprisoned in the abbey, and also to seize all the students that had been concerned in the riot and bring them to London. The earl proceeded to execute his commission. He apprehended thirty of the students, and, taking them to a neighboring castle, he shut them up there as prisoners.

In the end, besides punishing the individual students who had made this disturbance, the regents and masters of the University were compelled to come to London, and there to go barefooted through the principal street to a church where the legate was, and humbly to supplicate his forgiveness for the indignity which he had suffered. And so, with great difficulty, they obtained their pardon.

The students in those days, as students are apt to be in all countries and in all ages, were a very impulsive, and, in some respects, a lawless set. Whenever they deemed themselves injured, they pursued the object of their hostility in the most reckless and relentless manner. At one time a member of the University became so excited against the king on account of some injury, real or imaginary, which he had suffered, that he resolved to kill him. So he feigned himself mad, and in this guise he loitered many days about the palace of Woodstock, where the king was then residing, until at length he became well acquainted with all the localities. Then, watching his opportunity, he climbed by night through a window into a bedchamber where he thought the king was lying. He crept up to the bedside, and, throwing back the clothes, he stabbed several times into the bed with a dagger. He, however, stabbed nothing but the bed itself, and the pillow, for the king that night, as it happened, lay in another chamber.

As the student was making his escape, he was spied by one of the chambermaids named Margaret Biset. Margaret immediately made a great outcry, and the other servants, coming up, seized the student and carried him off to prison. He was afterward tried, and was convicted of treason in having made an attempt upon the king's life, and was hanged. Before his death he said that he had been employed to kill the king by another man, a certain William de Marish, who was a noted and prominent man of those days. This William de Marish was afterward taken and brought to trial, but he solemnly denied that he had ever instigated the student to commit the crime. He was, however, condemned and executed, and, according to the custom in those days in the case of persons convicted of treason, his body was subjected after his death to extreme indignities, and then was divided into four quarters, one of which was sent to each of the four principal cities of the kingdom, and publicly exhibited in them as a warning to all men of the dreadful consequences of attempting such a crime.

Great pains were taken in those days to instill into the minds of all men the idea that to kill a king was the worst crime that a human being could commit. One of the writers of the time said that in wounding and killing a prince a man was guilty of homicide, parricide, Christicide, and even of deicide, all in one; that is, that in the person of a king slain by the hand of the murderer the criminal strikes not only at a man, but at his own father, and at Christ his Savior, and God.

A great many strange and superstitious notions were entertained by the people in respect to kings. These superstitions were encouraged, even by the scholars and historians of those times, who might be supposed to know better. But it was so much for their interest to write what should be agreeable to the king and to his court, that they were by no means scrupulous in respect to the tales which they told, provided they were likely to be pleasing to those in authority, and to strengthen the powers and prestige of the reigning families.

* * *

The neighboring countries with which the kings of England were most frequently at war in those days were Scotland, Wales, and France. These wars arose, not from any causes connected with the substantial interests of the people of England, but from the grasping ambition of the kings, who wished to increase the extent of their territories, and thus add to their revenues and to their power. Sometimes their wars arose from private and personal quarrels, and in these cases thousands of lives were often sacrificed, and great sums of money expended to revenge slights or personal injuries of comparatively little consequence.

For instance, one of the wars with Wales broke out in this manner. Leolin, who was then the reigning Prince of Wales, sent to France, and requested the King of France that he might have in marriage a certain lady named Lady Eleanor, who was then residing in the French king's court. The motive of Leolin in making this proposal was not that he bore any love for the Lady Eleanor, for very likely he had never seen her; but she was the daughter of an English earl named Montfort, Earl of Leicester, who was an enemy of the King of England, and, having been banished from the country, had taken refuge in France. Leolin thought that by proposing and carrying into effect this marriage, he would at once gratify the King of France and spite the King of England.

The King of France at once assented to the proposed marriage, but the King of England was extremely angry, and he determined to prevent the marriage if he could. He accordingly gave the necessary orders, and the little fleet which was sent from France to convey Eleanor to Wales was intercepted off the Scilly Islands on the way, and the whole bridal party were taken prisoners and sent to London.

As soon as Leolin heard this, he, of course, was greatly enraged, and he immediately set off with an armed troop, and made a foray upon the English frontiers, killing all the people that lived near the border, plundering their property, and burning up all the towns and villages that came in his way. There followed a long war. The English were, on the whole, the victors in the war, and at the end of it a treaty was made by which Leolin's wife, it is true, was restored to him, but his kingdom was brought almost completely under the power of the English kings.

Of course, Leolin was extremely dissatisfied with this result, and he became more and more uneasy in the enthralled position to which the English king had reduced him, and finally a new war broke out. Leolin was beaten in this war too, and in the end, in a desperate battle that was fought among the mountains, he was slain. He was slain near the beginning of the battle. The man who killed him did not know at the time who it was that he had killed, though he knew from his armor that he was some distinguished personage or other. When the battle was ended this man went back to the place to see, and, finding that it was the Prince Leolin whom he had slain, he was greatly pleased. He cut off the head from the body, and sent it as a present to the king. The king sent the head to London, there to be paraded through the streets on the end of a long pole as a token of victory. After being carried in this manner through Cheapside—then the principal street of London—in order that it might be gazed upon by all the people, it was set up on a high pole near the Tower, and there remained a long time, a trophy, as the king regarded it, of the glory and renown of a victory, but really an emblem of cruel injustice and wrong perpetrated by a strong against a weaker neighbor.

Not long after this the King of England succeeded in taking Prince David, the brother of Leolin, and, under the pretense that he had been guilty of treason, he cut off his head too, and set it up on another pole at the Tower of London, by the side of his brother's.

It must be admitted, however, that, although these ancient warriors were generally extremely unjust in their dealings with each other, and often barbarously cruel, they were still sometimes actuated by high and noble sentiments of honor and generosity. On one occasion, for instance, when this same Edward the First, who was so cruel in his treatment of Leolin, was at war in Scotland, and was besieging a castle there, he wrote one day certain dispatches to send to his council in London, and, having inquired for a speedy and trusty messenger to send them by, a certain Welshman named Lewin was sent to him. The king delivered the package to Lewin inclosed in a box, and also gave him money to bear his expenses on the way, and then sent him forth.

Lewin, however, instead of setting out on his journey, went to a tavern, and there, with a party of his companions, he spent the money which he had received in drink, and passed the night carousing. In the morning he said that he must set out on his journey, but before he went he must go back to the castle and have one parting shot at the garrison. Under this pretext, he took his cross-bow and proceeded toward the castle wall; but when he got there, instead of shooting his arrows, he called out to the wardens whom he saw on guard over the gate, and asked them to let down a rope and draw him up into the castle, as he had something of great importance to communicate to the governor of it.

So the wardens let down a rope and drew Lewin up, and then took him to the governor, who was then at breakfast. Lewin held out the box to the governor, saying,

"Here, sir, look in this box, and you may read all the secrets of the King of England."

He said, moreover, that he would like to have the governor give him a place on the wall, and see whether he could handle a cross-bow or not against the English army.

Gunpowder and guns had not been introduced as means of warfare at this time; the most formidable weapon that was then employed was the cross-bow. With the cross-bow a sort of square-headed arrow was used called a *quarrel*.

The governor, instead of accepting these offers on the part of Lewin, immediately went out to one of the turrets on the wall, and, calling to the English soldiers whom he saw below, he directed them to tell the King of England that one of his servants had turned traitor, and had come into the castle with a box of dispatches.

"And tell him," said the governor, "that if he will send some persons here to receive him, I will let the man down to them over the wall, and also restore the box of dispatches, which I have not opened at all."

Immediately Lord Spencer, one of the king's chief officers, came to the wall, and the governor of the castle let Lewin down to him by a rope, and also passed the box of letters down. The King of England was so much pleased with this generosity on the part of the governor that he immediately ceased his operations against the castle, though he caused Lewin to be hanged on a gallows of the highest kind.

* * *

But to return to Wales. After the death of Leolin and his brother the kingdom of Wales was annexed to England, and has ever since remained a possession of the British crown. The King of England partly induced the people of Wales to consent to this annexation by promising that he would still give them a native of Wales for prince. They thought he meant by this that they should continue to be governed by one of their own royal family; but what he really meant was that he would make his own son Prince of Wales. This son of his was then an infant. He was born in Wales. This happened from the fact that the king, in the course of his conquests in that country, had seized upon a place called Caernarvon, and had built a castle there, in a beautiful situation on the Straits of Menai, which separate the main land from the isle of Anglesea.

When his castle was finished the king brought the queen to Caernarvon to see it, and while she was there, her child, Prince Edward, who afterward became Edward the Second, was born.

This was the origin of the title of Prince of Wales, which has been held ever since by the oldest sons of the English sovereigns.

THE HISTORY OF RICHARD THE SECOND

Caernarvon Castle

This first English Prince of Wales led a most unhappy life, and his history illustrates in a most striking manner one of the classes of quarrels enumerated at the head of this chapter, namely, the disputes and contentions that often prevailed between the sovereign of the country and his principal nobles. While he was a young man he formed a very intimate friendship with another young man named Piers Gaveston. This Gaveston was a remarkably handsome youth, and very prepossessing and agreeable in his manners, and he soon gained a complete ascendency over the mind of young Edward. He was, however, very wild and dissolute in his habits, and the influence which he exerted upon Edward was extremely bad. As long as the common people only were injured by the lawless behavior of these young men, the king seems to have borne with them; but at last, in a riot in which they were concerned, they broke into the park of a bishop, and committed damage there which the king could not overlook. He caused his son, the young prince, to be seized and put into prison, and he banished Gaveston from the country, and forbade his son to have any thing more to do with him. This was in 1305, when the prince was twenty-one years of age.

In 1307, two years later, the king died, and the prince succeeded him, under the title of King Edward the Second. He immediately sent for Gaveston to return to England, where he received him with the greatest joy. He made him a duke, under the title of Duke of Cornwall; and as for the bishop whose park he and Gaveston had broken into, and on whose complaint Gaveston had been banished, in order to punish him for these offenses, the young king seized him and delivered him into Gaveston's hands as a prisoner, and at the same time confiscated his estates and gave them to Gaveston. Gaveston sent the bishop about from castle to castle as a prisoner, according as his caprice or fancy dictated.

These things made the barons and nobles of England extremely indignant, for Gaveston, besides being a corrupt and dissipated character, was, in fact, a foreigner by birth, being a native of Gascony, in France. His character seemed to grow worse with his exaltation, and he and Edward spent all their time in rioting and excess, and in perpetrating every species of iniquity.

Edward had been for some time engaged to be married to the Princess Isabel, the daughter of the King of France. About six months after his accession to the throne he set off for France to be married. It was his duty, according to the ancient usages of the realm, to appoint some member of the royal family, or some prominent person from the ancient nobility of the country, to govern the kingdom as regent during his absence; but instead of this he put Gaveston in this place, and clothed him with all the powers of a viceroy.

Edward was married to Isabel in Paris with great pomp and parade. Isabel was very beautiful, and was a general favorite. It is said that there were four kings and three queens present at the marriage ceremony. Edward, however, seemed to feel very little interest either in his bride or in the occasion of his marriage, but manifested a great impatience to get through with the ceremonies, so as to return to England and to Gaveston. As soon as it was possible, he set out on his return.

The bridal party were met at their landing by Gaveston, accompanied by all the principal nobility, who came to receive and welcome them at the frontier. The king was overjoyed to see Gaveston again. He fell into his arms, hugged and kissed him, and called him his dear brother, while, on the other hand, he took very little notice of the nobles and high officers of state. Everybody was surprised and displeased at this behavior, but as Edward was king there was nothing to be said or done.

Portrait of Edward the Second

Soon afterward the coronation took place, and on this occasion all the honors were allotted to Gaveston, to the utter neglect of the ancient and hereditary dignitaries of the realm. Gaveston carried the crown, and walked before the king and queen, and acted in all respects as if he were the principal personage in the country. The old nobles were, of course, extremely indignant at this. Hitherto they had expressed their displeasure at the king's favoritism by private murmurings and complaints, but now, they thought, it was time to take some concerted public action to remedy the evil; so they met together, and framed a petition to be sent to the king, in which, though under the form of a request, they, in fact, demanded that Gaveston should be dismissed from his offices, and required to leave the country.

The king was alarmed. He, however, could not think of giving his favorite up. So he said that he would return them an answer to the petition by-and-by, and he immediately began to pursue a more conciliatory course toward the nobles. But the effect of his attempts at conciliation was spoiled by Gaveston's behavior. He became more and more proud and ostentatious every day. He appeared in all public places, and every where he took precedence of the highest nobles of the land, and prided himself on outshining them in the pomp and parade which he displayed. He attended all the jousts and tournaments, and, as he was really a very handsome and well-formed man, and well skilled in the warlike sports in fashion in those days, he bore away most of the great prizes. He thus successfully rivaled the other nobles in gaining the admiration of the ladies of the court and the applause of the multitude, and made the nobles hate him more than ever.

Things went on in this way worse and worse, until at last the general sentiment became so strong against Gaveston that the Parliament, when it met, took a decided stand in opposition to him, and insisted that he should be expelled from the country. A struggle followed, but the king was obliged to yield. Gaveston was required to leave the country, and to take an oath never to return. It was only on these conditions that the Parliament would uphold the government, and thus the king saw that he must lose either his friend or his crown.

Gaveston went away. The king accompanied him to the sea-shore, and took leave of him there in the most affectionate manner, promising to bring him back again as soon as he could possibly do it. He immediately began to manoeuvre for the accomplishment of this purpose. In the mean time, as Gaveston had only sworn to leave *England*, the king sent him to Ireland, and made him governor general of that country, and there Gaveston lived in greater power and splendor than ever.

At length, in little more than a year, Gaveston came back. His oath not to return was disposed of by means of a dispensation which King Edward obtained for him from the Pope, absolving him from the obligation of it. When he was reinstated in the king's court he behaved more scandalously than ever. He revenged himself upon the nobles who had been the means of sending him away by ridiculing them and giving them nicknames. One of them he called Joseph the Jew, because his face was pale and thin, and bore, in some respects, a Jewish expression. Another, the Earl of Warwick, he called the Black Dog of Ardenne.

When the earl heard of this, he said, clenching his fist, "Very well; I'll make him feel the Black Dog's teeth yet."

In a word, the nobles were excited to the greatest pitch of rage and indignation against the favorite, and, after various struggles and contentions between them and the king, they at length broke out into an open revolt. The king at this time, with Gaveston and his wife, were at Newcastle, which is in the north of England. The barons fell upon him here with the intention of seizing Gaveston. Both the king and Gaveston, however, succeeded in making their escape. Gaveston fled to a castle, and shut himself up there. The king escaped by sea, leaving his wife behind, at the mercy of the conspirators. The barons treated the queen with respect, but they pressed on at once in pursuit of Gaveston. They laid siege to the castle where he sought refuge. Finding that the castle could not hold out long, Gaveston thought it best to surrender while it yet remained in his power to make terms with his enemies; so he agreed to give himself up, they stipulating that they would do him no bodily harm, but only confine him, and that the place of his confinement should be one of his own castles.

When he came down into the court-yard of the castle, after signing this stipulation, he found there ready to receive him the Earl of Warwick, the man to whom he had given the nickname of the Black Dog of Ardenne. The earl was at the head of a large force. He immediately took Gaveston into custody, and galloped off with him at the head of his troop to his own castle. The engraving represents a view of this fortress as it appeared in those days.

When they had got Gaveston safe into this castle, the chiefs held a sort of council of war to determine what should be done with their prisoner. While they were consulting on the subject, intending apparently to spare his life as they had agreed, some one called out,

"It has cost you a great deal of trouble to catch the fox, and now, if you let him go, you will have a great deal more trouble in hunting him again."

This consideration decided them; so they took the terrified prisoner, and, in spite of his piteous cries for mercy, they hurried him away to a solitary place a mile or two from the castle, and there, on a little knoll by the side of the road, they cut off his head.

Warwick Castle

One would have supposed that by this time the king would have been cured of the folly of devoting himself to favorites, but he was not. He mourned over the death of Gaveston at first with bitter grief, and when this first paroxysm of his sorrow was passed, it was succeeded with a still more bitter spirit of revenge. He immediately took the field against his rebellious barons, and a furious civil war ensued. He soon, too, found a new favorite, or, rather, two favorites. They were brothers, and their names were Spencer. They are called in history the Spencers, or the Despensers. The quarrels and wars which took place between the king and these favorites on one hand, and the barons and nobles on the other, were continued for many years. The queen took sides with the nobles against her husband and the Spencers. She fled to France, and there formed an intimacy with a young nobleman named Mortimer, who joined himself to her, and thenceforth accompanied her and made common cause with her against her husband. With this Mortimer she raised an army, and, sailing from Flanders, she landed in England. On landing, she summoned the barons to join her, and took the field against her husband. The king was beaten in this war, and fled again on board a vessel, intending to make his escape by sea. The two Spencers, one after the other, were taken prisoners, and both were hung on gibbets fifty feet high. They were hung in their armor, and after they were dead their bodies were taken down and treated as it was customary to treat the bodies of traitors. [In cases of treason the condemned man was first disemboweled; then his head was taken off; then the body was cut into quarters. The head and the four quarters of the body were then sent to various parts of the kingdom, and set up in conspicuous places in large cities and towns.]

In the midst of these proceedings the barons held a sort of Parliament, and made a solemn declaration that the king, by his flight, had abdicated the throne, and they proclaimed his son, the young Prince of Wales, then about fourteen years old, king, under the title of Edward the Third. In the mean time, the king himself, who had attempted to make his escape by sea, was tossed about in a storm for some days, until at last he was driven on the coast in South Wales. He concealed himself for some days in the mountains. Here he was hunted about for a time, until he was reduced to despair by his destitution and his sufferings, when at length he came forth and delivered himself up to his enemies.

He was made prisoner and immediately sent to Kenilworth Castle, and there secured. Afterward he was brought to trial. He was accused of shameful indolence and incapacity, and also of cowardice, cruelty, and oppression, and of having brought the country, by his vices and maladministration, to the verge of ruin. He was convicted on these charges, and the queen, his wife, confirmed the verdict.

Kenilworth Castle

Not being quite sure, after all, that by these means the dethronement of the king was legally complete, the Parliament sent a solemn deputation to Kenilworth Castle to depose the monarch in form. The king was brought out to meet this deputation in a great hall of the castle. He came just as he was, dressed in a simple black gown. The deputation told him that he was no longer king, that all allegiance had been withdrawn from him on the part of the people, and that henceforth he must consider himself as a private man. As they said this, the steward of the household came forward and broke his white wand, the badge of his office, in token that the household was dissolved, and he declared that by that act all the king's servants were discharged and freed. This was a ceremony that was usually performed at the death of a king, and it was considered in this case as completely and finally terminating the reign of Edward. The delegation also exacted from him something which they considered as a resignation of the crown. His son, the young prince, it was said, was unwilling to ascend the throne unless the barons could induce his father voluntarily to abdicate his own rights to it. They were the more desirous in this case of completely and forever extinguishing all of King Edward's claims, because they were afraid that there might be a secret party in his favor, and that that party might gain strength, and finally come out openly against them in civil war, in which case, if they were worsted, they knew that they would all be hung as traitors.

Indeed, soon after this time it began to appear that there were, in fact, some persons who were disposed to sympathize with the king. His queen, Isabel, who had been acting against him during the war, was now joined with Mortimer, her favorite, and they two held pretty much the whole control of the government, for the new king was yet too young to reign. Many of the monks and other ecclesiastics of the time openly declared that Isabel was guilty of great sin in thus abandoning her husband for the sake of another man. They said that she ought to leave Mortimer, and go and join her husband in his prison. And it was not long before it began to be rumored that secret plots were forming to attempt the king's deliverance from his enemies. This alarmed the nobles more than ever. The queen and some others wrote sharp letters to the keepers of the castle for dealing so gently with their prisoner, and gave them hints that they ought to kill him. In the end, the fallen monarch was transported from one fortress to another, until at length he came to Berkeley Castle. The inducement which led Mortimer and the queen to send the king to these different places was the hope that some one or other of the keepers of the castles would divine their wishes in regard to him, and put him to death. But no one did so. The keeper of Berkeley Castle, indeed, instead of putting his prisoner to death, seemed inclined to take compassion on him, and to treat him more kindly even than the others had done. Accordingly, after waiting some time, Mortimer seized an opportunity when Lord

A Monk of Those Days

Berkeley, having gone away from home, was detained away some days by sickness, to send two fierce and abandoned men, named Gourney and Ogle, to the castle, with instructions to kill the king in some way or other, but, if possible, in such a manner as to make it appear that he died a natural death. These men tried various plans without success. They administered poisons, and resorted to various other diabolical contrivances. At last, one night, dreadful outcries and groans were heard coming from the king's apartment. They were accompanied from time to time with shrieks of terrible agony. These sounds were continued for some time, and they were heard in all parts of the castle, and in many of the houses of the town. The truth was, the executioners whom Mortimer had sent were murdering the king in a manner almost too horrible to be described. The people in the castle and in the town knew very well what these dreadful outcries meant. They were filled with consternation and horror at the deed, and they spent the time in praying to God that he would receive the soul of the unhappy victim.

Berkeley Castle

After this, Mortimer and the queen for two or three years held pretty nearly supreme power in the realm, though, of course, they governed in the name of the young king, who was yet only fourteen or fifteen years of age. There was, however, a great secret hatred of Mortimer among all the old nobility of the realm. This ill-will ripened at last into open hostility. A conspiracy was formed to destroy Mortimer, and to depose the queen-mother from her power, and to place young Edward in possession of the kingdom. Mortimer discovered what was going on, and he went for safety, with Edward and the queen, to the castle of Nottingham, where he shut himself up, and placed a strong guard at the gates and on the walls.

This castle of Nottingham was situated upon a hill, on the side of which was a range of excavations which had been made in a chalky stone by some sort of quarrying. There was a subterranean passage from the interior of one of these caves which led to the castle. The castle itself was strongly guarded, and every night Isabel required the warden, on locking the gates, to bring the keys to her, and she kept them by her bedside. The governor of the castle, however, made an agreement with Lord Montacute, who was the leader in the conspiracy against Mortimer, to admit him to the castle at night through the subterranean passage. It seems that Mortimer and the queen did not know of the existence of this communication. They did not even know about the caves, for the mouths of them were at that time concealed by rubbish and brambles.

It was near midnight when Montacute and the party who went with him entered the passage. They crowded their way through the bushes and brambles till they found the entrance of the cave, and then went in. They were all completely armed, and they carried torches to light their way. They crept along the gloomy passage-way until at last they reached the door which led up into the interior of the castle. Here the governor was ready to let them in. As soon as they entered, they were joined by young Edward at the foot of the main tower.

Caves in the Hill-Side at Nottingham Castle

They left their torches here, and Edward led them up a secret staircase to a dark chamber. They crept softly into this room and listened. They could hear in an adjoining hall the voices of Mortimer and several of his adherents, who were holding a consultation. They waited a few minutes, and then, making a rush into the passage-way which led to the hall, they killed two knights who were on sentry there to guard the door, and, immediately bursting into the apartment, made Mortimer and all his friends prisoners.

The queen, who was in her bed in an adjoining room at this time, rushed frantically out when she heard the noise of the affray, and, with piteous entreaties and many tears, she begged and prayed Edward, her "sweet son," as she called him, to spare the gentle Mortimer, "her dearest friend, her well-beloved cousin." The conspirators did spare him at that time; they took him prisoner, and bore him away to a place of safety. He was soon afterward brought to trial on a charge of treason, and hanged. Isabel was deprived of all her property, and shut up in a castle as a prisoner of state. In this castle she afterward lived nearly thirty years, in lonely misery, and then died. The adjoining engraving represents a near view of the subterranean passage by which Lord Montacute and his party gained admission to the castle of Nottingham. It is known in modern times as "Mortimer's Hole."

Mortimer's Hole

3

The Black Prince

A.D. 1336-1346

Parentage of the Black Prince, Richard's father.—Reason for the name.—Situation of Crecy.—Nature of Edward's claim to the crown of France.—The Salic law.—Reason for it.—Edward's case.—Edward raises an army and sets out for France.—Map.—The army reaches Rouen.—Progress of the army.—Arrival at Amiens.—Progress of the two armies down the Somme.—Edward's anxiety about crossing the river.—Danger from the tide.—Edward posts himself at Crecy.—Plan of the battle.—The Black Prince in command.—Picture of the Genoese archer.—Philip gets out of patience.—The rain.—The battle.—More difficulty with the archers.—They send for help for the Prince of Wales.—Flight of the King of France from the field of battle.—Account of the old King of Bohemia.—Origin of the motto and device of the Prince of Wales.—Fate of Calais.—The six citizens.—Margaret of Calais.—John of Gaunt.

THE father of King Richard the Second was a celebrated Prince of Wales, known in history as the Black Prince. The Black Prince, as his title Prince of Wales implies, was the oldest son of the King of England. His father was Edward the Third. The Black Prince was, of course, heir to the crown, and he would have been king had it not happened that he died before his father. Consequently, when at last his father, King

Edward, died, Richard, who was the oldest son of the prince, and, of course, the grandson of the king, succeeded to the throne, although he was at that time only ten years old.

The Christian name of the Black Prince was Edward. He was called the Black Prince on account of the color of his armor. The knights and warriors of those days were often named in this way from some peculiarity in their armor.

Edward, being the oldest son of the king his father, was Prince of Wales. He was often called the Prince of Wales, and often simply Prince Edward; but, inasmuch as there were several successive Edwards, each of whom was in his youth the Prince of Wales, neither of those titles alone would be a sufficiently distinctive appellation for the purposes of history. This Edward accordingly, as he became very celebrated in his day, and inasmuch as, on account of his dying before his father, he never became anything more than Prince of Wales, is known in history almost exclusively by the title of the Black Prince.

But, although he never attained to a higher title than that of prince, he still lived to a very mature age. He was more than forty years old when he died. He, however, began to acquire his great celebrity when he was very young: he fought at the great battle of Crecy, in France, as one of the principal commanders on the English side, when he was only about seventeen years old.

Crecy, or Cressy, as it is sometimes called, is situated on the banks of the River Somme, in the northeast part of France. The circumstances under which the battle in this place was fought are as follows. The King of England, Edward the Third, the father of the Black Prince, laid claim to the throne of France. The ground of his claim was that, through his grandmother Isabel, who was a daughter of the French king, he was the nearest blood-relation to the royal line, all the other branches of the family nearer than his own being extinct. Now the people of France were, of course, very unwilling that the King of England should become entitled to the French crown, and they accordingly made a certain Prince Philip the king, who reigned under the title of Philip the Sixth.

Philip was the nearest relative after Edward, and he derived his descent through males alone, while Edward, claiming, as he did, through his grandmother Isabel, came through a female line.

Now there was an ancient law prevailing in certain portions of France, called the Salic law, [The Salic law is very celebrated in history, and questions growing out of it gave rise, in ancient times, to innumerable wars. It derived its name from a tribe of people called *Saliens*, by whom it was first introduced.] by which female children were excluded from inheriting the possessions of their fathers. This principle was at first applied to the inheriting of private property, but it was afterward extended to rights and titles of all sorts, and finally to the descent of the crown of France. Indeed, the right to rule over a province or a kingdom was considered in those days as a species of property, which descended from father to child by absolute right, over which the people governed had no control whatever.

The chief reason why the Salic law was applied to the case of the crown of France was not, as it might at first be supposed, because it was thought in those days that women were not qualified to reign, but because, by allowing the crown to descend to the daughters of the king as well as to the sons, there was danger of its passing out of the country. The *princes* of the royal family usually remained in their own land, and, if they married at all, they married usually foreign princesses, whom they brought home to live with them in their native land. The *princesses*, on the other hand, when they grew up, were very apt to marry princes of other countries, who took them away to the places where they, the princes, respectively lived. If, now, these princesses were allowed to inherit the crown, and, especially, if the inheritance were allowed to pass through them to their children, cases might occur in which the kingdom of France might descend to some foreign-born prince, the heir, or the actual ruler, perhaps, of some foreign kingdom.

This was precisely what happened in Edward's case. The Salic law had not then been fully established. Edward maintained that it was not law. He claimed that the crown descended through Isabel to him. The

French, on the other hand, insisted on passing him by, and decided that Philip, who, next to him, was the most direct descendant, and whose title came through a line of males, should be king.

In this state of things Edward raised a great army, and set out for France in order to possess himself of the French crown. The war continued many years, in the course of which Edward fitted out several different expeditions into France.

It was in one of these expeditions that he took his son, the Black Prince, then only seventeen years of age, as one of his generals. The prince was a remarkably fine young man, tall and manly in form, and possessed of a degree of maturity of mind above his years. He was affable and unassuming, too, in his manners, and was a great favorite among all the ranks of the army.

The map on the following page shows the course of the expedition, and the situation of Crecy. The fleet which brought the troops over landed there on a cape a little to the westward of the region shown upon the map. From the place where they landed they marched across the country, as seen by the track upon the map, toward the Seine. They took possession of the towns on the way, and plundered and wasted the country.

They advanced in this manner until at length they reached the river opposite Rouen, which was then, as now, a very large and important town. It stands on the eastern bank of the river. On reaching Rouen, Edward found the French army ready to meet him. There was a bridge of boats there, and Edward had intended to cross the river by it, and get into the town of Rouen. He found, however, on his arrival opposite the town, that the bridge was gone. The French king had destroyed it. He then turned his course up the river, keeping, of course, on the western and southern side of the stream, and looking out for an opportunity to cross. But as fast as he ascended on one side of the river, Philip ascended on the other, and destroyed all the bridges before Edward's armies could get to them. In this way the two armies advanced, each on its own side of the river, until they reached the environs of Paris, the English burning and destroying everything that came in their way. There was a good deal of manoeuvring between the two armies near Paris, in the course of which Edward contrived to get across the river. He crossed at Poissy by means of a bridge which Philip had only partially destroyed. While Philip was away, looking out for his capital, Paris, which Edward was threatening, Edward hastened back to get possession of the bridge, repaired it, and marched his army over before Philip could return.

Map: Campaign of Crecy

Both armies then struck across the country toward the River Somme. Philip reached the river first. He crossed at Amiens, and then went down on the right or eastern bank of the river, destroying all the bridges on the way. Edward, when he reached the river, found no place to cross. He tried at Pont St. Remi, at Long, and at other places, but failed everywhere. In the meantime, while his own forces had gradually been diminishing, Philip's had been rapidly increasing. Philip now divided his force. He sent down one portion on the eastern side of the river to prevent the English from crossing. With the other portion he came back to the left bank, and began to follow Edward's army down toward the mouth of the river. Edward went on in this way as far as Oisemont, and here he began to find himself in great danger of being hemmed in by Philip's army in a corner between the river and the sea.

View of Rouen from the West Side of the River

He sent scouts up and down to try to find someplace where he could cross by a ford, as the bridges were all down; but no fording-place could be found. He then ordered the prisoners that he had taken to be all brought together, and he offered liberty and a large reward in money to any one of them that would show him where there was a ford by which he could get his army across the river. He thought that they, being natives of the country, would be sure to know about the fording-places, if any there were. One of the prisoners, a countryman named Gobin, told him that there was a place a little lower down the river, called White Spot, where people could wade across the river when the tide was low. The tide ebbed and flowed in the river here, on account of its being so near the sea.

This was in the evening. King Edward was awake all night with anxiety, expecting every moment that Philip would come suddenly upon him. He rose at midnight, and ordered the trumpets to sound in order to arouse the men. The officers were all on the alert, the young prince among them. All was movement and bustle in the camp. As soon as the day dawned they commenced their march, Gobin leading the way. He was well guarded. They were all ready to cut him to pieces if he should fail to lead them to the ford which he had promised. But he found the ford, though at the time that the army reached the spot the tide was high, so that they could not cross. Besides this, the king saw that on the opposite bank there was a large body of French troops posted to guard the passage. Edward was obliged to wait some hours for the tide to go down, being in a terrible state of suspense all the time for fear that Philip should come down upon him in the rear, in which case his situation would have been perilous in the extreme.

At last the tide was low enough to make the river fordable, and Edward ordered his troops to dash forward into the river. The men advanced, but they were met in the middle of the stream by the troops that had been posted on the bank to oppose them. There was a short and desperate conflict in the water, but Edward at last forced his way through, and drove the French away.

It then required some hours for all his army to cross. They had barely time to accomplish the work before the tide came up again. Just at this time, too, Philip's army appeared, but it was too late for them to cross the ford, and so Edward escaped with the main body of his army, though a portion of those in the rear, who were not able to get across in time, fell into Philip's hands, and were either killed or taken prisoners on the margin of the water.

The young prince was, of course, as much rejoiced as his father at this fortunate escape. The army were all greatly encouraged, too, by the result of the battle which they had fought on the bank of the river in landing; and, finally, Edward resolved that he would not retreat any farther. He determined to choose a good position, and draw up his army in array, and so give Philip battle if he chose to come on. The place which he selected was a hill at Crecy. Philip soon after came up, and the battle was fought; and thus it was that Crecy became the scene of the great and celebrated conflict which bears its name.

King Edward arrayed his troops in successive lines on the declivity of the hill, while he himself took his station, with a large reserve, on the summit of it. He committed the general charge of the battle to his generals and knights, and one of the chief in command was the young prince, who was placed at the head of one of the most important lines, although he was at this time, as has already been said, only seventeen years old.

The King of France, with an immense host, came on toward the place where Edward was encamped, confident that, as soon as he could come up with him, he should at once overwhelm and destroy him. His army was very large, while Edward's was comparatively small. Philip's army, however, was not under good control. The vast columns filled the roads for miles, and when the front arrived at the place where Edward's army was posted, the officers attempted to halt them all, but those behind crowded on toward those in front, and made great confusion. Then there was disagreement and uncertainty among Philip's counselors in respect to the time of making the attack. Some were in favor of advancing at once, but others were for waiting till the next day, as the soldiers were worn out and exhausted by their long march.

There was a large body of Genoese archers who fought with cross-bows, a very heavy but a very efficient weapon. The officers who commanded these archers were in favor of waiting for the attack till the next day, as their men were very weary from the fatigue of carrying their cross-bows so far. They had marched eighteen miles that day, very heavily laden. Philip was angry with them for their unwillingness to go at once into battle.

"See," he cried out, "see what we get by employing such scoundrels, who fail us at the very moment when we want them."

This made the archers very angry, but nevertheless they formed in order of battle at the command of their officers, and went forward to the van. There went with them a large troop of horsemen under the French general. The horses of this troop were splendidly equipped, and were fierce for the fight.

While these preparations were making, a very black cloud was seen rising in the sky, until the whole heavens were darkened by it. The wind blew, and immense flocks of crows flew screaming

A Genoese Archer

through the air, over the heads of the army. Presently it began to rain. The rain increased rapidly, until it fell in torrents, and every body was drenched. There was, however, no possibility of shelter or escape from it, and the preparations for the fight accordingly still went on.

At length, about five o'clock, it cleared up, just as the battle was about to begin. The Genoese archers were in front with the horsemen, but the English, who had all this time remained calm and quiet at their posts, poured such a volley of arrows into their ranks that they were soon broken and began to be thrown into confusion. Other English soldiers ran out from their ranks armed with knives set into the ends of long poles, and they thrust these knives into the horses of the troop. The horses, terrified and maddened with the pain, turned round and ran in among the Genoese archers, and trampled many of them under foot. This made the whole body of archers waver and begin to fall back.

Then Philip, who was coming on behind at the head of other bodies of troops, fell into a great rage, and shouted out in a thundering voice,

"Kill me those scoundrels, for they only stop our way without doing any good."

Of course, this made the confusion worse than ever. In the mean time, the English soldiers, under the command of Prince Edward and the other leaders, pressed slowly and steadily forward, and poured in such an incessant and deadly fire of darts and arrows upon the confused and entangled masses of their enemies, that they could not rally or get into order again. Some of the French generals made desperate efforts in other parts of the field to turn the tide, but in vain.

At one time, when the battle was very hot in the part of the field where the young English prince was fighting, messengers went up the hill to the place where the king was stationed, near a wind-mill, whence he was watching the progress of the fight, to ask him to send some succor to the troops that were fighting with the prince.

"Is my son killed?" asked the king.

"No, sire," said the messenger.

"Is he unhorsed or wounded?" asked the king.

"No, sire," replied the messenger. "He is safe thus far, and is fighting with his troop, but he is very hard beset."

"No matter for that," said the king. "Go and tell him he can not have any help from me. I intend that the glory of this victory shall be for him alone, and for those to whom I have intrusted him."

Things went on in this way for some time, until at length the whole French army was thrown into utter confusion, and the men were flying in all directions. Night was coming on, and it was beginning to be impossible to distinguish friend from foe. A French knight rode up to the King of France, and, seizing his horse by the bridle, turned him away, saying to the king,

"Sire, it is time to withdraw. By remaining here any longer you will only sacrifice yourself to no purpose. Reserve yourself to win the victory some other day."

So the king turned and fled, a small party of his officers accompanying him. He fled to a castle in the neighborhood, called the Castle of La Broye, and sought refuge there. When the party arrived the gates were shut, for it was late and dark. They summoned the castellan, or keeper of the castle. He came out upon the battlements and demanded who was there.

The king called out,

"Open, castellan, open. It is the fortune of France."

The castellan knew the king's voice, and ordered the gate to be opened, and the drawbridge to be let down. The king and his party, which consisted of only five persons, went in. They remained at the castle only a short time to take some wine and other refreshment, and then set out again, at midnight, with guides furnished them by the castellan, and rode to Amiens, which, being a large and well-fortified town, was at least a temporary place of safety.

But, though the king himself thus made his escape, a great many of the knights and generals in his army would not fly, but remained fighting on the field until they were killed. There was one of the king's allies, the King of Bohemia, whose death, if the legends which have come down to us respecting this battle are true, occurred under very extraordinary circumstances. He was present with the army, not as a combatant, for he was old and blind, and thus completely helpless. He came, it would seem, to accompany his son, who was an active commander in Philip's army. His son was dangerously wounded, and forced to abandon the field, and the old king was so overwhelmed with chagrin at the result of the battle, and so enraged at the fate of his son, that he determined to charge upon the enemy himself. So he placed himself between two knights, who interlaced the bridle of his horse with the bridles of theirs, for the king himself could not see to guide the reins, and in this manner they rode into the thickest of the fight, where the Black Prince was contending. They were all almost immediately killed.

Prince Edward was so much struck with this spectacle, that he adopted the motto on the old king's shield for his. This motto was the

German phrase *Ich dien*, under three plumes. The words mean *I serve*. This motto and device have been borne in the coat of arms of the Prince of Wales from that day to this.

At the close of the battle the soldiers kindled up great fires on account of the darkness of the night, and in the light of them King Edward came down from his post on the hill, his heart full of exultation and joy at the greatness of the victory which his army had achieved, and at the glory of his son. In front of the whole army, he took his son in his arms and kissed him, and said,

"My dear son, God give you grace to persevere as you have begun. You are my true son, for loyally you have acquitted yourself this day, and well do you deserve a crown."

Edward received these honors in a very modest and unassuming manner. He bowed reverentially before his father, and attributed to others rather than to himself the success of the day. His modesty and generosity of demeanor, connected with the undaunted bravery which he had really evinced in the fight, caused the whole army to feel an enthusiastic admiration for him, and, as fast as tidings of these events extended, all Europe was filled with his fame.

After gaining this great battle Edward marched to Calais, a very important sea-port on the coast, to the northward of the mouth of the Somme, and laid siege to that town; and, although it was so strongly fortified that he could not force his way into it, he succeeded at length in starving the inhabitants into a surrender. He was so exasperated at the obstinate resistance of the people, that at last, when they were ready to surrender, he declared that he would only spare their lives on condition that six of the principal inhabitants should come out to his camp barefooted, bareheaded, and with halters about their necks, in order that they might be hung immediately. These cruel terms were complied with. Six of the principal inhabitants of the town volunteered to give themselves up as victims. They proceeded to Edward's camp, but their lives were saved by the interposition of Philippa, the queen, Prince Edward's mother. The king was exceedingly unwilling to spare them, but he could not resist the entreaties of Philippa, though he said he wished she had been somewhere else, so as not to have interfered with his revenge.

Edward and all his army, with the queen and Prince Edward, marched into Calais with great pomp and parade. Soon after their entrance into the town a daughter was born to Philippa, who was called, from the place of her nativity, Margaret of Calais.

Besides this sister Margaret, Prince Edward had a brother born on the Continent of Europe. His name was John, and he was born in Ghent. He was called John of Ghent, or, as the English historians generally wrote it, John of Gaunt.

After the taking of Calais there were other campaigns and battles, and more victories, some upon one side and some upon the other; and then, when both parties were so exhausted that their strength was gone, while yet their hostility and hate continued unappeased, a truce was made. Then after the truce came new wars, and thus years rolled on. During all this time the Black Prince distinguished himself greatly as one of the chief of his father's generals. He grew up to full manhood; and while, like the other warlike chieftains of those days, his life was devoted to deeds of rapine and murder, there was in his demeanor toward those with whom he was at peace, and toward enemies who were entirely subdued, a certain high-toned nobleness and generosity of character, which, combined with his undaunted courage, and his extraordinary strength and prowess on the field of battle, made him one of the greatest lights of chivalry of his age.

4

The Battle of Poictiers

A.D. 1356-1360

The Black Prince sets out for France.—Plymouth.—The ships of those days. —The prince ravages the country.—Progress of the Black Prince.—The country laid waste.—The King of France comes to meet the Black Prince. —Ambuscade near Romorantin.—Reconnoitring party.—The English troop surprised.—The French surprised in their turn.—The French retreat to the castle.—The castle besieged.—Crossing the ditch.—Engines.—The castle taken.—King John and his four sons.—Attempt of the Pope's legate to make peace.—Negotiations of the Pope's legate.—The English camp.— The cardinal obtains a truce.—The king's pavilion.—King John's demands.—Prince Edward will not yield to them.—Story of the two knights. —Coats of arms.—Quarrel between the two knights.—Preparations for the battle.—English position.—The horses and the barbed arrows.—The English victorious.—Fate of the king's sons.—The victory announced to the prince.—The men called in.—Gathering at the prince's tent.—Two barons sent to look for the king.—The King of France and his son taken prisoners.—Quarrel about them.—The two barons take possession of the prisoners.—Denys.—His previous adventures.—The king's surrender to him.—Prince Edward makes a supper for his prisoners.—Generous demeanor of the prince.—Disposition of the prisoners.—English prisoners.— Douglas's extraordinary escape from his captors.—Prince Edward conveys the King of France to London.—Entrance into London.—Magnanimous treatment of the prisoner.—The war ended.—The king ransomed.—Prince Edward's renown.—Edward the heir apparent to the crown.

IN process of time, Philip, the King of France, against whom these wars had been waged, died, and John succeeded him. In the course of the reign of John, the Black Prince, when he was about twenty-five years of age, set out from England, at the head of a large body of men, to invade France on the southern and western side. His first destination was Gascony, a country in the southern part of France, between the Garonne, the Pyrenees, and the sea.

From London he went to Plymouth, where the fleet had been assembled in which he was to sail. He was accompanied on his march by an immense number of nobles and barons, all splendidly equipped and armed, and full of enthusiastic expectations of the glory which they were to acquire in serving in such a campaign, under so famed and brilliant a commander.

The fleet which awaited the army at Plymouth consisted of three hundred vessels. The expedition was detained for a long time in the port, waiting for a fair wind and good weather. At length the favorable time arrived. The army embarked, and the ships set sail in sight of a vast assemblage, formed by people of the surrounding country, who crowded the shores to witness the spectacle.

The ships of those times were not large, and, judging from some of the pictures that have come down to us, they were of very odd construction. On the adjoining page is a copy of one of these pictures, from an ancient manuscript of about this time.

These pictures, however, are evidently intended rather as *symbols* of ships, as it were, than literally correct representations of them. Still, we can deduce from them some general idea of the form and structure actually employed in the naval architecture of those times.

Ancient Representation of English Ships

Prince Edward's fleet had a prosperous voyage, and his army landed safely in Gascony. Soon after landing he commenced his march through the country to the eastward, pillaging, burning, and destroying wherever he went. The inhabitants of the country, whom the progress of his march thus overwhelmed with ruin, had nothing whatever to do with the quarrel between his father and the King of France. It made very little difference to them under whose reign they lived. It is not at all unlikely that far the greater portion of them had never even heard of the quarrel. They were quietly engaged in their various industrial pursuits, dreaming probably of no danger, until the advance of this army, coming upon them mysteriously, no one knew whither, like a plague, or a tornado, or a great conflagration, drove them from their homes, and sent them flying about the country in all directions in terror and despair. The prince enjoyed the credit and the fame of being a generous and magnanimous prince. But his generosity and magnanimity were only shown toward knights, and nobles, and princes like himself, for it was only when such as these were the objects of these virtues that he could gain credit and fame by the display of them.

In this march of devastation and destruction the prince overran all the southern part of France. One of his attendants in this campaign, a knight who served in the prince's household, in a letter which he wrote back to England from Bordeaux, gave the following summary of the results of the expedition:

> "My lord rode thus abroad in the countrie of his enimies eight whole weekes, and rested not past eleven daies in all those places where he came. And know it for certeine that since this warre began against the French king, he had neuer such losse or destruction as he hath had in this iournie; for the countries and good townes which were wasted in this iournie found to the King of France euerie yeare more to the maintainance of his warre than half his realme hath doon beside, except, &c.

"My lord rode thus abroad in the countrie of his enimies eight whole weekes and rested not past eleven daies in all those places where he came. And know it for certeine that since this warre began against the French king, he had never such losse or destruction as he hath had in this journie; for the countries and good townes which were wasted in this journie found to the King of France everie yeare more to the maintainance of his warre than half his realme hath doon beside, except, &c."

THE HISTORY OF RICHARD THE SECOND

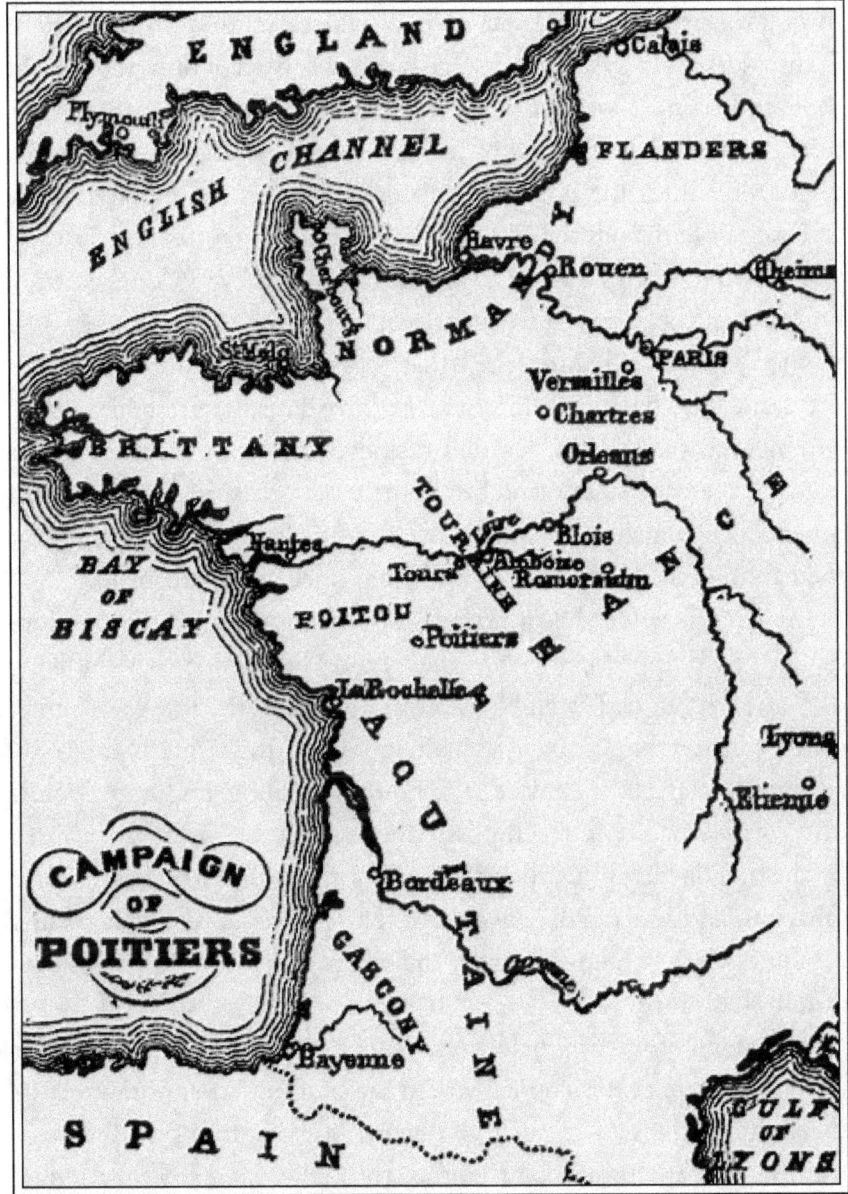

Map—Campaign of Poictiers

After having thus laid waste the southern coast, the prince turned his course northward, toward the heart of the country, carrying devastation and destruction with him wherever he came. He advanced through Auvergne and Berri, two provinces in the central part of France. His army was not very large, for it consisted of only about eight thousand men. It was, however, very compact and efficient, and the prince advanced at the head of it in a very slow and cautious manner. He depended for the sustenance of his soldiers on the supplies which he could obtain from the country itself. Accordingly, he moved slowly from town to town, so as not to fatigue his soldiers by too long marches, nor exhaust them by too frequent battles. "When he was entered anie towne," says the old chronicler, "that was sufficientlie stored of things necessarie, he would tarrie there two or three daies to refresh his soldiers and men of warre, and when they dislodged they would strike out the heads of the wine vessels, and burne the wheat, oats, and barlie, and all other things which they could not take with them, to the intent that their enimies should not therewith be sustained and nourished."

At length, while the prince was advancing through the province of Berri, and approaching the River Loire, he learned that the King of France, John, had assembled a great army at Paris, and was coming down to meet him. Large detachments from this army had already advanced as far as the banks of the Loire, and all the important points on that river had been taken possession of, and were strongly guarded by them. The king himself, at the head of the main force, had reached Chartres, and was rapidly advancing. The prince heard this news at a certain castle which he had taken, and where he had stopped some days to refresh his men.

A council of war was held to determine what should be done. The prevailing voice at this council was in favor of not attempting to cross the Loire in the face of such an enemy, but of turning to the westward toward the province of Poitou, through which a way of retreat to the southward would be open in case a retreat should be necessary. The prince determined to accept this advice, and so he put his army in motion toward the town of Romorantin.

Now the King of France had sent a detachment of his troops, under the command of three famous knights, across the Loire. This detachment consisted of about three hundred horsemen, all armed from head to foot, and mounted on swift chargers. This squadron had been hovering in the neighborhood of the English army for some days, watching for an opportunity to attack them, but without success. Now, foreseeing that Edward would attempt to enter Romorantin, they pushed forward in a stealthy manner to the neighborhood of that town, and placed themselves in ambush at the sides of a narrow and solitary gorge in the mountains, through which they knew the English must necessarily pass.

On the same day that the French knights formed this ambush, several of the commanders in Edward's army asked leave to take a troop of two hundred men from the English army, and ride forward to the gates of the town, in order to reconnoitre the place, and ascertain whether the way was clear for the main body of the army to approach. Edward gave them permission, and they set forward. As might have been expected, they fell into the snare which the French knights had laid for them. The Frenchmen remained quiet and still in their hiding-places, and allowed the English to pass on through the defile. Then, as soon as they had passed, the French rushed out and galloped after them, with their spears in their rests, all ready for a charge.

The English troop, hearing the sound of the galloping of horses in the road behind them, turned round to see what was coming. To their dismay, they found that a troop of their enemies was close upon them, and that they were hemmed in between them and the town. A furious battle ensued. The English, though they were somewhat fewer in number than the French, seem to have been made desperate by their danger, and they fought like tigers. For a time it was uncertain which way the contest would turn, but at length, while the victory was still undecided, the van of the main body of the English army began to arrive upon the ground. The French now saw that they were in danger of being overpowered with numbers, and they immediately began to retreat. They fled in the direction of the town. The English followed them in a headlong pursuit, filling the air with their shouts, and with the clanking of their iron armor as the horses galloped furiously along.

At length they reached the gates of the town, and the whole throng of horsemen, pursuers and pursued, pressed in together. The French succeeded in reaching the castle, and, as soon as they got in, they shut the gates and secured themselves there, but the English got possession of the town. As soon as Edward came in, he sent a summons to the people in the castle to surrender. They refused. Edward then ordered his men to prepare for an assault on the following day.

Accordingly, on the following day the assault was made. The battle was continued all day, but without success on the part of the assailants, and when the evening came on Edward was obliged to call off his men.

Storming of the Castle of Romorantin

The next morning, at a very early hour, the men were called to arms again. A new assaulting force was organized, and at sunrise the trumpet sounded the order for them to advance to the attack. Prince Edward himself took the command at this trial, and by his presence and his example incited the men to make the greatest possible efforts to batter down the gates and to scale the walls. Edward was excited to a high degree of resentment and rage against the garrison of the castle, not only on account of the general obstinacy of their resistance, but because, on the preceding day, a squire, who was attendant upon him, and to whom he was strongly attached, was killed at his side by a stone hurled from the castle wall. When he saw this man fall, he took a solemn oath that he would never leave the place until he had the castle and all that were in it in his power.

But, notwithstanding all the efforts of his soldiers, the castle still held out. Edward's troops thronged the margin of the ditch, and shot arrows so incessantly at the battlements that the garrison could scarcely show themselves for an instant on the walls. Finally, they made hurdles and floats of various kinds, by means of which large numbers succeeded, half by swimming and half by floating, to get across the ditch, and then began to dig in under the wall, while the garrison attempted to stop their work by throwing down big stones upon their heads, and pots of hot lime to eat out their eyes.

At another part the besiegers constructed great engines, such as were used in those days, in the absence of cannon, for throwing rocks and heavy beams of wood, to batter the walls. These machines also threw a certain extraordinary combustible substance called Greek fire. It was this Greek fire that, in the end, turned the scale of victory, for it caught in the lower court of the castle, where it burned so furiously that it baffled all the efforts of the besieged to extinguish it, and at length they were compelled to surrender. Edward made the principal commanders prisoners, but he let the others go free. The castle itself he utterly destroyed.

Having thus finished this work, Edward resumed his march, passing on to the westward through Touraine, to avoid the French king, who he knew was coming down upon him from the direction of Chartres at the head of an overwhelming army. King John advanced to the Loire, and sending different detachments of his army to different points, with orders to cross at any bridges that they could find, he himself came to Blois, where he crossed the river to Amboise, and thence proceeded to

Loches. Here he learned that the English were moving off to the westward, through Touraine, in hopes to make their escape. He set off after them at full speed.

He had four sons with him in his army, all young men. Their names were Charles, Louis, John, and Philip.

At length the two armies began to approach each other near the town of Poictiers.

In the meantime, while the crisis had thus been gradually approaching, the Pope, who was at this time residing at Avignon in France, sent one of his cardinals to act as intercessor between the belligerents, in hopes of bringing them to a peace. At the time when the two armies had drawn near to each other and the battle seemed imminent, the cardinal was at Poictiers, and just as the King of France was marshaling his troops in the order of battle, and preparing for the onset, the cardinal, at the head of his suite of attendants, galloped out to the king's camp, and, riding up to him at full speed, he begged him to pause a moment that he might speak to him.

The king gave him leave to speak, and he thus began.

"Most dear sire," said he, "you have here with you a great and powerful army, commanded by the flower of the knighthood of your whole kingdom. The English, compared with you, are but a handful. They are wholly unable to resist you. You can make whatever terms with them you please, and it will be far more honorable and praiseworthy in you to spare their lives, and the lives of your gallant followers, by making peace with them on such terms as you may think right, without a battle, than to fight with them and destroy them. I entreat you, therefore, sire, that before you proceed any farther, you will allow me to go to the English camp to represent to the prince the great danger he is in, and to see what terms you can make with him."

"Very well," replied the king. "We have no objection. Go, but make haste back again."

The cardinal immediately set off, and rode with all speed into the English camp. The English troops had posted themselves at a spot where they were in a great measure concealed and protected among hedges, vineyards, and groves. The cardinal advanced through a narrow lane, and came up to the English prince at last, whom he found in a vineyard. The prince was on foot, and was surrounded by knights and armed men, with whom he was arranging the plan of the battle.

The prince received the cardinal very graciously, and heard what he had to say. The cardinal represented to him how overwhelming was the force which the King of France had brought against him, and how imminent the danger was that he and all his forces would be totally destroyed in case of a conflict, and urged him, for the sake of humanity as well as from a proper regard for his own interest, to enter into negotiations for peace.

Prince Edward replied that he had no objection to enter into such negotiations, and that he was willing to accept of terms of peace, provided his own honor and that of his army were saved.

The cardinal then returned to the King of France, and reported to him what the prince had said, and he entreated the king to grant a truce until the next morning, in order to afford time for the negotiations.

The knights and barons that were around the king were very unwilling that he should listen to this proposal. They were fierce for the battle, and could not brook the idea of delay. But the cardinal was so urgent, and he pleaded so strongly and so eloquently for peace, that, finally, the king yielded.

"But we will not leave our posts," said he. "We will remain on the ground ready for the onset to-morrow morning, unless our terms are accepted before that time."

So they brought the royal tent, which was a magnificent pavilion of red silk, and pitched it on the field for the king. The army were dismissed to their quarters until the following day.

The time when this took place was early in the morning. The day was Sunday. During all the rest of the day the cardinal was employed in riding back and forth between the two armies, conveying proposals and counter-proposals, and doing all in his power to effect an arrangement.

But all his efforts were unsuccessful. King John demanded that four of the principal persons in Edward's army should be given up unconditionally to his will, and that the whole army should surrender themselves as prisoners of war. This Prince Edward would not consent to. He was willing, he said, to give up all the French prisoners that he had in custody, and also to restore all the castles and towns which he had taken from the French. He was also willing to bind himself for seven years not to take up arms against the King of France. But all this did not satisfy John. He finally offered that, if the prince would surrender himself and one hundred knights as prisoners of war, he would let the rest of the army go free, and declared that that was his ultimatum. Prince Edward positively refused to accept any such conditions, and so the cardinal, greatly disappointed at the failure of his efforts, gave up the case as hopeless, and returned with a sad and sorrowful heart to Poictiers.

An anecdote is related in this connection by one of the ancient chroniclers, which illustrates curiously some of the ideas and manners of those times. During the course of the day, while the truce was in force, and the cardinal was going back and forth between the two armies, parties of knights belonging to the two encampments rode out from time to time from their own quarters along the lines of the enemy, to see what was to be seen. In these cases they sometimes met each other, and held conversation together, both parties being bound in honor by the truce not to commit any act of hostility. There was a certain English knight, named Sir John Chandos, who in this way met a French knight named Clermont. Both these knights were mounted and fully armed. It was the custom in those days for each knight to have something peculiar in the style of his armor to distinguish him from the rest, and it was particularly the usage for each one to have a certain device and motto on his shield, or on some other conspicuous position of his clothing. These devices and mottoes are the origin of the *coats of arms* in use at the present day.

It happened that the device of these two knights was nearly the same. It consisted of a representation of the Virgin Mary embroidered in blue, and surrounded by a radiance of sunbeams. Clermont, on perceiving that the device of Chandos was so similar to his own, called out to him when he came near, demanding,

"How long is it, sir, since you have taken the liberty to wear my arms?"

"It is you yourself who are wearing mine," said Chandos.

"It is false," replied Clermont; "and if it were not for the truce, I would soon show you to whom that device rightfully belongs."

"Very well," replied Chandos. "To-morrow, when the truce is over, you will find me on the field ready to settle the question with you by force of arms."

With that the angry noblemen parted, and each rode back to his own lines.

Early on Monday morning both armies prepared for battle. The cardinal, however, being extremely unwilling to give up all hope of preventing the conflict, came out again, at a very early hour, to the French camp, and made an effort to renew the negotiations. But the king peremptorily refused to listen to him, and ordered him to be gone. He would not listen, he said, to any more pretended treaties or pacifications. So the cardinal perceived that he must go away, and leave the armies to their fate. He called at Prince Edward's camp and bade him farewell, saying that he had done all in his power to save him, but it was of no avail. He then returned to Poictiers.

The two armies now prepared for battle. The King of France clothed himself in his royal armor, and nineteen of his knights were armed in the same manner, in order to prevent the enemy from being able to single out the king on the field. This was a common stratagem employed on such occasions. The English were strongly posted on a hill side, among vineyards and groves. The approach to their position was through a sort of lane bordered by hedges. The English archers were posted along these hedges, and when the French troops attempted to advance, the archers poured such a shower of barbed arrows into the horses' sides, that they soon threw them into confusion. The barbed arrows could not be withdrawn, and the horses, terrified with the stinging pain, would rear, and plunge, and turn round upon those behind them, until at length the lane was filled with horses and horsemen piled together in confusion. Now, when once a scene of confusion like this occurred upon a field of battle, it was almost impossible to recover from it, for the iron armor which these knights wore was so heavy and so cumbersome, that when once they were unhorsed they could not mount again, and sometimes could not even rise, but writhed and struggled helplessly on the ground until their squires came to relieve them.

The battle raged for many hours, but, contrary to the universal expectation, the English were every where victorious. Whether this was owing to the superior discipline of the English troops, or to the reckless desperation with which their situation inspired them, or to the compact disposition that the prince had made of his forces, or to the shelter and protection afforded by the trees, and hedges, and vines, among which they were posted, or to the superior talents of the Black Prince as a commanding officer, or to all these causes combined, it is impossible to say. The result was, however, that the French were every where overcome, thrown into confusion, and put to flight. Three of the French king's sons were led off early from the field, their attendants excusing their flight by their anxiety to save the princes from being taken prisoners or put to death. A large squadron were driven off on the road to Poictiers. The inhabitants of Poictiers, seeing them coming, shut the gates to keep them out, and the horsemen, pursuers and pursued, became jammed together in a confused mass at the gates, and on the causeway leading to them, where they trampled upon and killed each other by hundreds. In every other direction, too, detached portions of the two armies were engaged in desperate conflicts, and the air was filled with the clangor of arms, the notes of the trumpets, the shouts of the victors, and the shrieks and groans of the wounded and dying.

At length Sir John Chandos, who had fought in company with Prince Edward all the day, advanced to the prince, and announced to him that he thought the battle was over.

"Victory!" said he, "victory! The enemy is beaten and driven wholly off the ground. It is time to halt and to call in our men. They are getting greatly scattered. I have taken a survey of the ground, and I do not see any where any French banners flying, or any considerable bodies of French troops remaining. The whole army is dispersed."

So the king gave orders to halt, and the trumpets blew the signal for the men to cease from the pursuit of their enemies, and to gather again around the prince's banner. They set up the banner upon a high bush, near where the prince was standing, and the minstrels, gathering around it, began to play in honor of the victory, while the trumpets in the distance were sounding to recall the men.

The officers of the prince's household brought the royal tent, a beautiful pavilion of crimson silk, and pitched it on the spot. They brought wine, too, and other refreshments; and as the knights, and barons, and other noble warriors arrived at the tent, the prince offered them refreshments, and received their congratulations on the great deliverance which they had achieved. A great many prisoners were brought in by the returning knights to be held for ransom.

While the knights and nobles were thus rejoicing together around the prince's tent, the prince asked if any one knew what had become of the King of France. No one could answer. So the prince dispatched two trusty barons to ride over the field and see if they could learn any tidings of him. The barons mounted their horses at the door of the pavilion and rode away. They proceeded first to a small hillock which promised to afford a good view. When they reached the top of this hillock, they saw at some distance a crowd of men-at-arms coming along together at a certain part of the field. They were on foot, and were advancing very slowly, and there seemed to be some peculiar excitement among them, for they were crowding and pushing each other in a remarkable manner. The truth was, that the men had got the King of France and his youngest son Philip in their possession, and were attempting to bring them in to the prince's tent, but were quarreling among themselves as they came along, being unable to decide which of them was entitled to the custody of the prisoners. The barons immediately put spurs to their horses, and galloped down the hill to the spot, and demanded what was the matter. The people said that it was the King of France and his son who had been made prisoners, and that there were no less than ten knights and squires that claimed them. These men were wrangling and contending together with so much violence and noise that there was danger that the king and the young prince would be pulled to pieces by them. The king, in the mean time, was entreating them to be quiet, and begging them to deal gently with them, and take them at once to Prince Edward's tent.

"Gentlemen, gentlemen," said he, "I pray you to desist, and conduct me and my son in a courteous manner to my cousin the prince, and do not make such a riot about us. There will be ransom enough for you all."

The contending knights and barons, however, paid little heed to these words, but went on vociferating, "It is *I* that took him."

"I tell you he is *my* prisoner."

"No, no, *we* took him. Let him alone. He belongs to *us*."

The two barons pressed their horses forward into the midst of the crowd, and drove the knights back. They ordered them all, in the name of the prince, to let go the prisoners and retire, and they threatened to cut down on the spot any man who refused to obey. The barons then dismounted, and, making a profound reverence before the king, they took him and his son under their protection, and conducted them to the prince's tent.

The prince received the royal prisoners in the kindest and most respectful manner. He made a very low obeisance to the king, and treated him in every respect with the utmost consideration. He provided him with every thing necessary for his comfort, and ordered refreshments to be brought, which refreshments he presented to the king himself, as if he were an honored and distinguished guest instead of a helpless prisoner.

Although there were so many English knights and barons who claimed the honor of having made the King of France prisoner, the person to whom he really had surrendered was a French knight named Denys. Denys had formerly lived in France, but he had killed a man in a quarrel there, and for this crime his property had been confiscated, and he had been banished from the realm. He had then gone to England, where he had entered into the service of the king, and, finally, had joined the expedition of the Prince of Wales. This Denys happened to be in the part of the field where the King of France and his son Philip were engaged. The king was desperately beset by his foes, who were calling upon him all around in English to surrender. They did not wish to kill him, preferring to take him prisoner for the sake of the ransom. The king was not willing to surrender to any person of inferior rank, so he continued the struggle, though almost overpowered. Just then Denys came up, and, calling out to him in French, advised him to surrender. The king was much pleased to hear the sound of his own language, and he called out,

"To whom shall I surrender? Who are you?"

"I am a French knight," said Denys; "I was banished from France, and I now serve the English prince. Surrender to me."

"Where is the prince?" said the king. "If I could see him I would speak to him."

"He is not here," said Denys; "but you had better surrender to me, and I will take you immediately to the part of the field where he is."

So the king drew off his gauntlet, and gave it to Denys as a token that he surrendered to him; but all the English knights who were present crowded around, and claimed the prisoner as theirs. Denys attempted to conduct the king to Prince Edward, all the knights accompanying him, and struggling to get possession of the prisoner by the way. It was while the contention between Denys and these his competitors was going on, that the two barons rode up, and rescued the king and his son from the danger they were in.

* * *

That night Prince Edward made a sumptuous supper for the king and his son. The tables were spread in the prince's pavilion. The greater part of the French knights and barons who had been taken prisoners were invited to this banquet. The king and his son, with a few French nobles of high rank, were placed at an elevated table superbly appointed and arranged. There were side tables set for the squires and knights of lower degree. Prince Edward, instead of seating himself at the table with the king, took his place as an attendant, and served the king while he ate, notwithstanding all the entreaties of the king that he would not do so. He said that he was not worthy to sit at the table of so great a king and of so valiant a man as the king had shown himself to be that day.

In a word, in all his demeanor toward the king, instead of triumphing over him, and boasting of the victory which he had achieved, he did everything in his power to soothe and assuage the fallen monarch's sorrow, and to diminish his chagrin.

"You must not allow yourself to be dejected, sire," said he, "because the fortune of war has turned against you this day. By the manner in which you acquitted yourself on the field, you have gained imperishable renown; and though, in the decision of divine Providence, the battle has gone against you for the moment, you have nothing personally to fear either for yourself or for your son. You may rely with perfect confidence upon receiving the most honorable treatment from my father. I am sure that he will show you every attention in his power, and that he will arrange for your ransom in so liberal and generous a spirit that you and he will henceforth become warm and constant friends."

This kind and respectful treatment of his prisoners made a very strong impression upon the minds of all the French knights and nobles, and they were warm in their praises of the magnanimity of their victorious enemy. He treated these knights themselves, too, in the same generous manner. He liberated a large number of them on their simple promise that they would send him the sums which he named respectively for their ransoms.

Although Edward was thus, on the whole, victorious in this battle, still many of the English knights were killed, and quite a number were taken prisoners and carried off by the French to be held for ransom. One of these prisoners, a Scotch knight named Douglas, made his escape after his capture in a very singular manner. He was standing in his armor among his captors late in the evening, at a place at some distance from the field, where the French had taken him and some other prisoners for safety, and the French were about to take off his armor, which, from its magnificence, led them to suppose that he was a person of high rank and importance, as he really was, and that a grand ransom could be obtained for him, when another Scotch knight, named Ramsay, suddenly fixing his eyes upon him, pretended to be in a great rage, and, advancing toward him, exclaimed,

"You miserable wretch! How comes it that you dare to deck yourself out in this way in your master's armor? You have murdered and robbed him, I suppose. Come here and pull off my boots."

Douglas understood at once Ramsay's design, and so, with pretended tremblings, and looks of guilt and fear, he came to Ramsay and pulled off one of his boots. Ramsay took up the boot and struck Douglas upon the head with it. The other English prisoners, wondering, asked Ramsay what he meant.

"That is Lord Douglas," said they.

"Lord Douglas?" repeated Ramsay, in a tone of contempt. "No such thing. It is his servant. He has killed his master, I suppose, and stolen his armor." Then, turning to Douglas and brandishing the boot over him again, he cried out,

"Off with you, you villain! Go and look over the field, and find your master's body, and when you have found it come back and tell me, that I may at least give him a decent burial."

So saying, he took out forty shillings, and gave the money to the Frenchmen as the ransom of the pretended servant, and then drove Douglas off, beating him with the boot and saying,

"Away with you! Begone!"

Douglas bore this all very patiently, and went away with the air of a detected impostor, and soon got back safely to the English camp.

***

After the battle of Poictiers Prince Edward moved on toward the westward with his army, taking with him his royal prisoners, and stopping at all the large towns on his way to celebrate his victory with feastings and rejoicings. At last he reached Bordeaux on the coast, and from Bordeaux, in due time, he set sail with his prisoners for London. In the mean time, news of the victory, and of the coming of the King of France as prisoner to England, had reached London, and great preparations were made there for the reception of the prince. The prince took a fleet of ships and a large force of armed men with him on the voyage, being afraid that the French would attempt to intercept him and rescue the prisoners. The King of France and his suite had a ship to themselves. The fleet landed at a place called Sandwich, on the southern coast of England, and then the cortège of the prince proceeded by slow journeys to London.

The party was received at the capital with great pomp and parade. Besides the cavalcades of nobles, knights, and barons which came out to meet them, all the different trades and companies of London appeared in their respective uniforms, with flags and banners, and with the various emblems and insignia of their several crafts. All London flocked into the streets to see the show.

One would have supposed, however, from the arrangements which Prince Edward made in entering the city, that the person whom all this pomp and parade was intended to honor was not himself, but the king his captive; for, instead of riding at the head of the procession in triumph, with the King of France and his son following as captives in his train, he gave the king the place of honor, while he himself took the station of one of his attendants. The king was mounted on a white charger very splendidly caparisoned, while Prince Edward rode a small black horse by his side. The procession moved in this way through the principal streets of the city to a palace on the banks of the river at the West End, which had been fitted up in the most complete and sumptuous manner for the king's reception. Soon after this, the King of England, Prince Edward's father, came to pay his captive cousin a visit, and, though he retained him as a captive, he treated him in other respects with every mark of consideration and honor.

The King of France and his son remained captives in England for some time. The king and the queen treated them with great consideration. They often visited King John at his palace, and they invited him to the most sumptuous entertainments and celebrations made expressly to do him honor.

In the mean time, the war between England and France still went on. Many battles were fought, and many towns and castles were besieged and taken. But, after all, no great progress was made on either side, and at length, when both parties had become wearied and exhausted in the struggle, a peace was concluded, and King John, having paid a suitable ransom for himself and for those who were with him, was allowed to return home. He had been in captivity for about five years.

* * *

The conduct of Prince Edward at the battles of Crecy and of Poictiers, in both which contests the English fought against an immense superiority of numbers, and the great eclat of such an achievement as capturing the French king, and conducting him a prisoner to London, joined to the noble generosity which he displayed in his treatment of his prisoners, made his name celebrated throughout the world. Everybody was sounding the praises of the Black Prince, the heir apparent to the English throne, and anticipating the greatness and glory to which England would attain when he should become king.

This was an event which might occur at any time, for King Edward his father was drawing gradually into the later years of life, and he himself was now nearly forty years of age.

5

Childhood of Richard

A.D. 1366-1370

Prince Edward becomes Prince of Aquitaine.—Various calls made upon him.—Don Pedro.—Edward's plans and arrangements.—Lord D'Albret.—Lord D'Albret offers a thousand men.—King Edward offers his aid.—John of Gaunt.—Why the princess wishes to have Edward's departure postponed.—Prince Edward's letter to Lord D'Albret.—Lord D'Albret is very angry.—His determination.—Lord D'Albret's letter to the prince.—Edward in want of money.—Don Pedro pledges his three daughters.—The baptism of the young Prince Richard.—Richard receives a visit from his uncle John.—Richard at Bordeaux.—Don Pedro's troubles and perplexities.—King Charles determines to call Prince Edward to account.—The commissioners arrive, and are received by the prince.—The lawyer reads the letter.—The prince is very much displeased.—He dismisses the commissioners.—Indignation of the prince.—He wishes to arrest the commissioners.—The commissioners seized and imprisoned.—Death of Richard's brother.—The prince determines to go to England.—Prince Edward's farewell speech.—He sails for England.—Little Richard at sea.—Pleasant and prosperous voyage.—Portrait of Edward III.—Richard's first entrance into England.

THE HISTORY OF RICHARD THE SECOND

THE child of Edward the Black Prince, who afterward became Richard the Second, king of England, was born at Bordeaux, in the southwestern part of France, in the year 1367, in the midst of a scene of great military bustle and excitement. The circumstances were these.

When peace was finally made between England and France, after the wars described in the last chapter were over, one of the results of the treaty which was made was that certain provinces in the southwestern part of France were ceded to England, and formed into a principality called Aquitaine, and this principality was placed under the dominion of the Black Prince. The title of the prince was thenceforth not only Prince of Wales, but also Prince of Aquitaine. The city of Bordeaux, near the mouth of the Garonne, as shown by the map, was the chief city of Aquitaine. There the prince established his court, and reigned, as it were, for several years in great splendor. The fame which he had acquired attracted to his court a great number of knights and nobles from all lands, and whenever a great personage had any wrongs, real or imaginary, to be redressed, or any political end to gain which required the force of arms, he was very likely to come to the Prince of Aquitaine, in order, if possible, to secure his aid. Prince Edward was rather pleased than otherwise with these applications, for he loved war much better than peace, and, though he evinced a great deal of moderation and generosity in his conduct in the treatment of his vanquished enemies, he was none the less really excited and pleased with the glory and renown which his victories gained him.

About six months before Richard was born, while Edward was living with the princess, his wife, in Bordeaux, he received an application for aid from a certain Don Pedro, who claimed to be King of Navarre in Spain, but who had been expelled from his kingdom by his brother. There was also a certain James who claimed to be the King of Majorca, a large island in the Mediterranean Sea, who was in much the same situation in respect to *his* kingdom. Prince Edward promised to aid Don Pedro in recovering his throne, and he forthwith began to make preparations to this end. He also promised James that, as soon as he had accomplished the work which he had undertaken for Don Pedro, he would fit out an expedition to Majorca, and so restore him too to his kingdom.

The preparations which he made for the expedition into Spain were prosecuted in a very vigorous manner. Don Pedro was destitute of means as well as of men, and Edward was obliged to raise a large sum of money for the provisioning and paying of his troops. His vassals, the nobles and barons of his principality, were obliged to furnish the men, it being the custom in those times that each vassal should bring to his lord, in case of war, as many soldiers as could be spared from among his own tenants and retainers—some fifty, some one hundred, and some two hundred, or even more, according to the extent and populousness of their estates. One of the nobles in Prince Edward's service, named Lord D'Albret, had offered to bring a thousand men. The prince had asked him on some public occasion, in presence of other knights and noblemen, how many men he could furnish for the expedition.

"My lord," replied Lord D'Albret, "if you really wish for all the strength that I can furnish, I can bring you a thousand lances, and still have enough at home to guard the country."

The prince was surprised at this answer. He did not know, it seems, how powerful the barons of his principality were.

"By my head!" said he, addressing Lord D'Albret and speaking in French, which was, of course, the language of Aquitaine, "that will be very handsome."

He then turned to some English nobles who were near, and speaking in English, said it was worth while to rule in a country where one baron could attend his lord with a thousand lances. He was ashamed not to accept this offer, for, according to the ideas of these times, it would not be at all consistent with what was expected of a prince that he should not be able to maintain and pay as many troops as his barons could bring him. So he said hastily, turning to D'Albret, that he engaged them all.

Although, in the end, Don Pedro, if he succeeded in regaining his kingdom, was to refund the expenses of the war, yet, in the first instance, it was necessary for the prince to raise the money, and he soon found that it would be very difficult for him to raise enough. He was unwilling to tax too heavily the subjects of his principality, and so, after collecting as much as he thought prudent in that way, he sent to England to his father, explaining the nature and design of the proposed expedition, and soliciting his father's approval of it, and, at the same time, asking for aid in the way of funds. King Edward replied, cordially approving of the enterprise. He also promised to send on the prince's brother John, with a body of troops to accompany the expedition. This John was the one who has already been mentioned as born in Ghent, and who was called, on that account, John of Gaunt. He was also Duke of Lancaster, and is often designated by that name. Edward was very much attached to his brother John, and was very much pleased to hear that he was coming to join him.

The King of England also, Edward's father, made arrangements for sending to his son a large sum of money. This was of great assistance to him, but still he had not money enough. So he broke up his plate, both gold and silver, and caused it to be coined, in order to assist in filling his treasury. Still, notwithstanding all that he could do, he found it difficult to provide sufficient funds for the purchase of the provisions that he required, and for the pay of the men.

It was rather late in the season when the prince first formed the plan of this expedition. He was very anxious to set out as soon as possible, for he had the Pyrenees to cross, in order to pass from France into Spain, and it would be impossible, he knew, to conduct an army over the mountains after the winter should set in; so he hastened his preparations as much as possible. He was kept in a continued fever by his impatience, and by the various delays and disappointments which were constantly occurring. In the mean while, time moved on, and it began at length to be doubtful whether he should be ready to march before the winter should set in.

To add to his perplexity, his wife begged him to postpone his departure till the spring, in order that he might remain at home with her until after their child should be born. She was dejected in spirits, and seemed particularly sad and sorrowful at the thought of her husband's going away to leave her at such a time. She knew, too, the undaunted recklessness with which he was accustomed to expose himself to danger in his campaigns, and if he went away she could not but think that it was uncertain whether he would ever return.

Finally, the prince concluded to put off his departure until spring. This determination, however, in some sense increased his perplexities, for now he had a large proportion of his force to maintain and pay through the winter. This made it necessary that he should curtail his plans in some degree, and, among other things, he resolved to notify the Baron D'Albret not to bring his whole complement of one thousand men. It was a great humiliation to him to do this after having formally agreed to engage the men, but he felt compelled, by the necessity of the case, to do so, and he accordingly wrote to the baron the following letter:

"MY LORD D'ALBRET,

"Whereas, out of our liberal bounty, we have retained you, with a thousand lances, to serve under us in the expedition which, through the grace of God, we intend speedily to undertake and briefly to finish, having duly considered the business, and the costs and expenses we are at, we have resolved that several of our vassals should remain at home in order to guard the territories. For these causes, it has been determined in our council that you shall serve in this expedition with two hundred lances only. You will choose the two hundred out from the rest, and the remainder you will leave at home to follow their usual occupations.

"May God have you under his holy protection.

"Given at Bordeaux, the eighth day of December.

"EDWARD."

This letter was sealed with the great seal of the prince, and sent to D'Albret, who was in his own country, busily engaged in assembling and equipping his men, and making the other necessary preparations. The baron was exceedingly indignant when he received the letter. In those days, every man that was capable of bearing arms liked much better to be taken into the service of some prince or potentate going to war than to remain at home to cultivate the ground in quiet industry. D'Albret knew, therefore, very well, that his vassals and retainers would be all greatly disappointed to learn that four fifths of their whole number were, after all, to remain at home, and then, besides this, his own importance in the campaign would be greatly diminished by reducing the force under his command from one thousand to two hundred men. He was extremely angry when he read the letter.

"How is this?" he exclaimed. "My lord the Prince of Wales trifles with me when he orders me to disband eight hundred knights and squires whom, by his command, I have retained, and have diverted from other means of obtaining profit and honor." Then he called for a secretary, and said to him in a rage,

"Write what I shall dictate to you."

The secretary wrote as follows from his master's dictation:

"MY DEAR LORD,

"I am marvelously surprised at the contents of the letter which you have sent me. I do not know and can not imagine what answer I can make. Your present orders will do me a great injury, and subject me to much blame. For all the men-at-arms whom I have retained by your command have already made their preparations for entering your service, and were only waiting your orders to march. By retaining them for your service I have prevented them from seeking honor and profit elsewhere. Some of the knights had actually made engagements to go beyond sea, to Jerusalem, to Constantinople, or to Russia, in order to advance themselves, and now, having relinquished these advantageous prospects in order to join your enterprise, they will be extremely displeased if they are left behind. I am myself equally displeased, and I can not conceive what I have done to deserve such treatment. And I beg you to understand, my lord, that I cannot be separated from my men; nor will they consent to be separated from each other. I am convinced that, if I dismiss any of them, they will all go."

The baron added other words of the same tenor, and then, signing and sealing the letter, sent it to the prince. The prince was angry in his turn when he received this letter.

"By my faith," said he, "this man D'Albret is altogether too great a man for my country, when he seeks thus to disobey an order from my council. But let him go where he pleases. We will perform this expedition, if it please God, without *any* of his thousand lances."

This case presents a specimen of the perplexities and troubles in which the prince was involved during the winter, while organizing his expedition and preparing to set out in the spring. The want of money was the great difficulty, for there was no lack of men. Don Pedro agreed, it is true, that when he recovered his kingdom he would pay back the advances which Edward had to make, but he was so unprincipled a man that Edward knew very well that he could not trust to his promises unless he gave some security. So Don Pedro agreed to leave his three daughters in Edward's hands as hostages to secure the payment of the money.

The names of the three princesses thus pledged as collateral security for money borrowed were Beatrice, Constance, and Isabel.

At length, on the third day of April, the child was born. The princess was in a monastery at the time, called the monastery of St. Andrew, whither she had retired for privacy and quiet. Immediately after the event, Prince Edward, having made every thing ready before, gave orders that the expedition should set forward on the road to Spain. He himself was to follow as soon as the baptism of the child should be performed. The day on which the child was born was Wednesday, and Friday was fixed for the baptism. The baptism took place at noon, at a stone font in the church of the monastery. The King of Majorca, whom the prince had promised to restore to his kingdom, was one of the godfathers. The child was named Richard.

On the Sunday following the prince bade his wife and the little infant farewell, and set out from Bordeaux with great pomp, at the head of an immense cavalcade, and went on to join the expedition which was already on its way to Spain.

Richard Receiving the Visit of His Uncle John

The birth of Richard was an event of great importance, for he was not only the son of the Prince of Aquitaine, but he was the grandson of the King of England, and, of course, everyone knew that he might one day be the King of England himself. Still, the probability was not very great that this would happen, at least for a long period to come; for, though his father, Prince Edward, was the oldest son of the King of England, he himself was not the oldest son of his father. He had a brother who was some years older than himself, and, of course, there were three lives that must be terminated before his turn should come to reign in England—his grandfather's, his father's, and his brother's.

It happened that all these three lives *were* terminated in a comparatively brief period, so that Richard really became King of England before he grew up to be a man.

The first important occurrence which took place at the monastery at Bordeaux, where little Richard remained with his mother after his father had gone, was the arrival of his uncle John, that is, John of Gaunt, the Duke of Lancaster, who was on his way from England at the head of an army to accompany his brother into Spain. John stopped at Bordeaux to see the princess and the infant child. He was very joyfully received by the princess, and by all the ladies in attendance upon her. The princess was very fond of her brother, and she was much pleased that he was going to join her husband in the war in Spain; besides, he brought her late and full news from England. The duke, however, did not remain long at Bordeaux, but, after a brief visit to his sister, he put himself again at the head of his troops, and hurried forward to overtake the prince, who was already far on his way toward the Pyrenees and Spain.

Little Richard remained in Bordeaux for three or four years. During this time he had his brother for a playmate, but he saw little of his father. It was some time before his father returned from Spain, and when he did return he came home much depressed in spirits, and harassed and vexed with many cares. He had succeeded, it is true, in conquering Don Pedro's enemies, and in placing Don Pedro himself again upon the throne; but he had failed in getting back the money that he had expended. Don Pedro could not or would not repay him. What Prince Edward did with the three daughters of the king that had been left with him as hostages I do not know. At any rate, he could not pay his debts with them, or raise money by means of them to silence his clamorous troops. He attempted to lay fresh taxes upon the people of Aquitaine.

This awakened a great deal of discontent. The barons who had had disagreements of any sort with Edward before, took advantage of this discontent to form plots against him, and at last several of them, D'Albret among the rest, whom he had mortally offended by countermanding his orders for the thousand men, combined together and sent to the King of France, complaining of the oppressions which they suffered under Edward's rule, and inviting him to come and help them free themselves. The king at once determined that he would do this.

This King of France was, however, not King John, whom Edward had made prisoner and sent to London. King John had died, and the crown had descended to his successor, Charles the Fifth.

King Charles determined first to send two commissioners to summon the Prince of Aquitaine into his presence to give an account of himself. He did this under the pretext that Aquitaine was part of France, and that, consequently, Prince Edward was in some sense under his jurisdiction.

The two commissioners, with their attendants, left Paris, and set out on their journey to Bordeaux. People traveled very slowly in those days, and the commissioners were a long time on the way. At length, however, they reached Bordeaux. They arrived late in the evening, and took up their quarters at an inn. The next day they repaired to the monastery where the prince was residing.

They informed the attendants who received them at the monastery that they had been sent by the King of France with a message to the prince. The attendants, who were officers of the prince's court, informed the prince of the arrival of the strangers, and he ordered them to be brought into his presence.

The commissioners, on being brought before the prince, bowed very low in token of reverence, and presented their credentials. The prince, after reading the credentials, and examining the seals of the King of France by which they were authenticated, said to the commissioners,

"It is very well. These papers show that you are duly commissioned embassadors from the King of France. You are welcome to our court.

And you can now proceed to communicate the message with which you have been charged."

Of the two commissioners, one was a lawyer, and the other a knight. The knight bore the singular name of Caponnel de Caponnal. The lawyer, of course, was the principal speaker at the interview with the prince, and when the prince called for the communication which had been sent from the King of France, he drew forth a paper which he said contained what the King of France had to say, and which, he added, they, the commissioners, had promised faithfully to read in the prince's presence.

The prince, wondering greatly what the paper could contain, ordered the lawyer to proceed with the reading of it.

The lawyer read as follows:

> "Charles, by the grace of God, King of France, to our nephew the Prince of Wales and Aquitaine, health.
>
> "Whereas several prelates, barons, knights, universities, fraternities, and colleges of the country and district of Gascony, residing and inhabiting upon the borders of our realm, together with many others from the country and duchy of Aquitaine, have come before us in our court to claim justice for certain grievances and unjust oppressions which you, through weak counsel and foolish advice, have been induced to do them, and at which we are much astonished;
>
> "Therefore, in order to obviate and remedy such things, we do take cognizance of their cause, insomuch that we, of our royal majesty and sovereignty, order and command you to appear in our city of Paris in person, and that you show and present yourself before us in our chamber of Paris, to hear judgment pronounced upon the aforesaid complaints and grievances done by you to our subjects, who claim to be heard, and to have the jurisdiction of our court.

"Let there be no delay in obeying this summons, but set out as speedily as possible after having heard this order read.

"In witness whereof we have affixed our seal to these presents.

"Given at Paris the twenty-fifth day of January, 1369.

"CHARLES R."

On hearing this letter read, the prince was filled with astonishment and indignation. He paused a moment, with his eyes fixed upon the commissioners, as if not knowing what to reply. At length, with an expression of bitter irony upon his countenance, he said,

"We shall willingly appear at the appointed day at Paris, since the King of France sends for us, but it will be with our helmet on our head, and accompanied by sixty thousand men."

The commissioners, seeing how much the prince was displeased, began immediately to entreat him not to be angry with them as the bearers of the message.

"Oh no," said the prince, "I am not in the least angry with you, but only with those that sent you hither. Your master, the King of France, has been exceedingly ill advised in thus pretending to claim jurisdiction over our dominion of Aquitaine, and in taking the part of our discontented subjects against us, their rightful sovereign. When he surrendered the provinces to the King of England, my father, as he did by solemn treaty, he relinquished forever all jurisdiction over them, and in the exercise of my government I acknowledge no superior except my father. Tell the King of France that is what I claim and will maintain. It shall cost a hundred thousand lives before it shall be otherwise."

Having spoken these words in a calm and quiet, but very resolute and determined tone, the prince walked off out of the apartment, leaving the commissioners in a great state of astonishment and alarm. They seemed to know not what to do.

Some of the courtiers came to them and advised them to withdraw. "It is useless," said they, "for you to attempt any thing more. You have delivered your message faithfully, and the prince has given his answer. It is the only answer that he will give, you may depend, and you may as well return with it to the king."

So the messengers went back to the inn, and on the evening of the same day they set out on their return to Paris. In the mean time, Prince Edward continued to feel extremely indignant at the message which he had received. The more he reflected upon it, indeed, the more angry he became. He felt as if he had been insulted in having had such a summons from a foreign potentate served upon him by a lawyer in his own house. The knights and barons around him, sharing his anger, proposed that they should pursue and seize the commissioners, with a view of punishing them for their audacity in bringing such a message. At first the prince was unwilling to consent to this, as the persons of embassadors and messengers of all sorts sent from one sovereign to another were, in those days as now, considered sacred. At last, however, he said that he thought the men were hardly to be considered as the messengers of the King of France.

"They are virtually," said he, "the messengers of D'Albret and the other factious and rebellious barons among our own subjects, who complained to the King of France and incited him to interfere in our affairs, and, as such, I should not be sorry to have them taken and punished."

This was sufficient. The knights who heard it immediately sent off a small troop of horsemen, who overtook the commissioners before they reached the frontier. In order not to compromise the prince, they said nothing about having been sent by him, but arrested the men on a charge of having taken a horse which did not belong to them from the inn. Under pretense of investigating this charge, they took the men to a neighboring town and shut them up in a castle there.

Some of the attendants of the commissioners, who had come with them from France, made their escape, and, returning to Paris, they reported to the King of France all that had occurred. It now came his turn to be angry, and both parties began to prepare for war.

The King of England took sides with his son, and so was drawn at once into the quarrel. Various military expeditions were fitted out on both sides. Provinces were ravaged, and towns and castles were stormed. The Prince of Wales was overwhelmed with the troubles and perplexities which surrounded him. His people were discontented, his finances were low, and the fortune of war often turned against him. His health, too, began to fail him, and he sank into a state of great dejection and despondency. To complete the sum of his misfortunes, his oldest son, Richard's brother, fell sick and died. This was a fortunate event for Richard, for it advanced him to the position of the oldest surviving son, and made him thus his father's heir. It brought him, too, one step nearer to the English throne. Richard was, however, at this time only four years old, and thus was too young to understand these things, and probably, sympathizing with his father and mother, he mourned his brother's death. The parents, at any rate, were exceedingly grieved at the loss of their first-born child, and the despondency of the prince was greatly increased by the event.

At last the physicians and counselors of Edward advised that he should leave his principality for a time and repair to England. They hoped that by the change of scene and air he might recover his spirits, and perhaps regain his health. The prince resolved on following this advice. So he made arrangements for leaving his principality under the government and care of his brother, John of Gaunt, and then ordered a vessel to be made ready at Bordeaux to convey himself, the princess, and Richard to England.

When every thing was ready for his departure, he convened an assembly of all the barons and knights of his dominions in a hall of audience at Bordeaux, and there solemnly committed the charge of the principality to his brother John in the presence of them all.

He said in the speech that he made to them on that occasion, that during all the time that he had been their prince, he had always maintained them in peace, prosperity, and power, so far as depended on him, against all their enemies, and that now, in the hope of recovering his health, which was greatly impaired, he intended to return to England. He therefore earnestly besought them to place confidence in, and faithfully serve and obey, his brother, the Duke of Lancaster, as they had hitherto served and obeyed him.

The barons all solemnly promised to obey these injunctions, and they took the oath of fealty and homage to the duke. They then bid the prince farewell, and he soon afterward embarked on board the ship with his wife and son, and set sail for England.

The fleet which accompanied the prince on the voyage, as convoy to the prince's ship, contained five hundred men-at-arms, and a large body of archers besides. This force was intended to guard against the danger of being intercepted by the French on the way. The prince and the princess must, of course, have felt some solicitude on this account, but Richard, being yet only four years old, was too young to concern himself with any such fears. So he played about the ship during the voyage, untroubled by the anxieties and cares which weighed upon the spirits of his father and mother.

The voyage was a very prosperous one. The weather was pleasant and the wind was fair, and after a few days' sail the fleet arrived safely at Southampton. The king, with his family and suite, disembarked. They remained two days at Southampton to refresh themselves after the voyage, and to allow the prince, who seemed to be growing worse rather than better, a little time to gather strength for the journey to London. When the time arrived for setting out, he was found too ill to travel by any of the ordinary modes, and so they placed him upon a litter, and in this way the party set out for Windsor Castle.

The party traveled by easy stages, and at length arrived at the castle. Here Richard for the first time saw his grandfather, Edward the Third, King of England. They were all very kindly received by him. After remaining a short time at Windsor Castle, the prince, with his wife and Richard, and the knights, and barons, and other attendants who had come with him from Aquitaine, proceeded to a place called Birkhamstead, about twenty miles from London, and there took up his abode.

Portrait of Edward the Third, Richard's Grandfather

And thus it was that Richard for the first time entered the country which had been the land of his ancestors for so long a time, and over which he was himself so soon to reign.

6

Accession to the Throne

A.D. 1376

John of Gaunt.—His thoughts in respect to the kingdom.—Laws of succession.—Prince Edward grows worse.—He dies.—Grand burial of the prince at Canterbury.—Richard is declared heir to the crown.—Grand entertainment at Christmas.—Bad character of the king.—Alice Perrers. —Death of the king.—A council of government appointed.—Chivalry.— Fear of the French.—Embargo.—Some account of Wickliffe the reformer. —The Pope's bulls.—Meaning of the term.—The golden bull.—Trial of Wickliffe in London.—The assembly.—Violent disputes.—Rudeness of the Duke of Lancaster.—Indignation of the people.—Priest murdered.— Alarm of the mayor and aldermen.—Deputation sent to the young king. —The Londoners summoned.—Richard holds a court.—The whole difficulty amicably settled.

YOUNG RICHARD lived in comparative retirement with his mother for about six years after his return to England. His father's sickness continued. Indeed, the prince was so feeble in body, and so dejected and desponding in mind, that he was well-nigh incapable of taking any part in public affairs. His brother, John of Gaunt, Duke of Lancaster, remained for some time in Aquitaine, and was engaged in continual wars with France, but at length he too returned to England. He was a man of great energy of character and of great ambition, and he began to revolve the question in his mind whether, in case his brother, the Prince of Wales, should die, the inheritance of the kingdom of England should fall to him, or to Richard, the son of his brother.

"My brother Edward is older than I," he said to himself, "and if he should live till after our father the king dies, then I grant that he should succeed to the throne. But if he dies before the king, then it is better that I should succeed to the throne, for his son Richard is but a child, and is wholly unfit to reign. Besides, if the oldest son of a king is dead, it is more reasonable that the next oldest should succeed him, rather than that the crown should go down to the children of the one who has died."

The laws of succession were not absolutely settled in those days, so that, in doubtful cases, it was not uncommon for the king himself, or the Parliament, or the king and Parliament together, to select from among different claimants, during the life-time of the king, the one whom they wished to succeed to the crown.

All were agreed, however, in this case—the king, the Parliament, and the people of the country—that if Edward should survive his father, he was the rightful heir. He was a universal favorite, and people had been long anticipating a period of great prosperity and glory for the kingdom of England when he should be king.

In the mean time, however, his health grew worse and worse, and at length, in 1376, he died. His death produced a great sensation. Provision was made for a very magnificent funeral. The prince died at Westminster, which was then a mile or two west from London, though now London has become so extended that Westminster forms the west end of the town. It was determined to bury the prince in the Cathedral at Canterbury. Canterbury is in the south-eastern part of England, and was then, as now, the residence of the archbishop, and the religious metropolis, so to speak, of the kingdom. When the day of the funeral arrived, an immense cavalcade and procession was formed at Westminster. All the nobles of the court and the members of Parliament joined in the train as mourners, and followed the body through the city. The body was placed on a magnificent hearse, which was drawn by twelve horses. Immense throngs of people crowded the streets and the windows to see the procession go by. After passing through the city, the hearse, attended by the proper escort, took the road to Canterbury, and there the body of the prince was interred. A monument was erected over the tomb, upon which was placed an effigy of the prince, dressed in the armor in which the illustrious wearer had gained so many victories and acquired such lasting renown.

Edward, the Black Prince.

This engraving represents the effigy of the Black Prince, as now seen upon his monument on the north side of the Cathedral at Canterbury.

The King of France, although the prince had been one of his most implacable enemies all his life, and had been engaged in incessant wars against him, caused funeral solemnities to be celebrated in Paris on the occasion of his death.

The ceremonies were performed with great magnificence in the chapel of the royal palace, and all the barons, knights, and nobles of the court attended in grand costume, and joined in rendering honor to the memory of their departed foe.

It was about midsummer when Richard's father died. Richard's uncle, John of Gaunt, Duke of Lancaster, was in London, and he had a large party in his favor, though generally he was very unpopular in England. He had not yet openly claimed the right to inherit the crown, nor did anyone know positively that he intended to do so. In order to prevent, if possible, any dispute on this question, and to anticipate any movements which John might otherwise make to secure the crown to himself, the Parliament petitioned the king to bring the young Prince Richard before them, that they might publicly receive him, and recognize him formally as heir to the crown. This the king did. Richard was dressed in royal robes, and conveyed in great state to the hall where Parliament was convened. Of course, the spectacle of a boy of ten years old brought in this manner before so august an assembly excited universal attention. The young prince was received with great honor. A solemn oath of allegiance was taken by all present, including the members of the Parliament, the great officers of state, and a number of nobles of high rank, including the Duke of Lancaster himself. In this oath, the claims of Richard to succeed his grandfather as King of England were recognized, and those taking the oath bound themselves forever to maintain his rights against all who should ever call them in question.

At Christmas of that year the king gave a great entertainment to all the lords and nobles of his court. At this entertainment he gave Prince Richard the highest place, next to himself, putting his uncle John, and all his other uncles, below him. This was to signify that he was now the second person in the kingdom, and that his uncles must always henceforth yield precedence to him.

The king was now sixty-five years of age. His health was very infirm. It was made so, in great measure, by his mode of life, which was scandalous. He associated with corrupt men and women, who led him into great excesses. As the spring of the year came on he grew worse, but he would not abandon his evil habits. He lived at one of his palaces on the Thames, a short distance above London, near Richmond. His government fell into great disorder, but he did nothing to restrain or correct the evils that occurred. In a word, he was fast relapsing into utter imbecility.

There was a young woman, named Alice Perrers, who had for some time been the favorite of the king, and had openly lived with him, greatly to the displeasure of many of his people. She was now with him at his palace. The nobles and courtiers who had been in attendance upon the king, seeing that he was soon to die, began to withdraw from him, and leave him to his fate. They saw that there was nothing more to be obtained from him, and that, for their future prospects, they must depend on the favor of Prince Richard or of his uncle John. It is true that Richard's right to the succession had been acknowledged, but then he was yet a child, and it was supposed that his uncle John, being the next oldest son of the king, would probably be appointed regent until he should come of age. So the courtiers left the dying monarch to his fate, and went to court the favor of those who were soon to succeed to his power. Some went to the palace of the Duke of Lancaster; others proceeded to Kennington, where the prince and his mother were residing. The poor king found himself forsaken of all the world, and left to die neglected and alone. It is said that Alice Perrers was the last to leave him, and that she only remained after the rest for the sake of a valuable ring which he wore upon his finger, and which she wished to get away from him as soon as the dying monarch was too far gone to be conscious of the robbery.

The counselors and nobles, though they thus forsook the king, were not wholly unmindful of the interests of the kingdom. They assembled immediately after his death, and determined that during Richard's minority the government should be administered by a council, and they selected for this council twelve men from among the highest nobles of the land. They determined upon this plan rather than upon a regency because they knew that if a regent were appointed it would be necessary that the Duke of Lancaster should be the man, and they were unwilling to put the power into his hands, for fear that he would not surrender it when Richard should come of age.

Besides, it would be in his power, in case he had been appointed regent, to have caused Richard to be put to death in some secret way, if he chose to do so, and then, of course, the crown would, without dispute, pass next to him. It was not wholly unreasonable to fear this, for such crimes had often been committed by rival against rival in the English royal line. A man might be in those days a very brave and gallant knight, a model in the eyes of all for the unsullied purity of his chivalric honor, and yet be ready to poison or starve an uncle, or a brother, or a nephew, without compunction or remorse, if their rights or interests conflicted with his own. The honor of chivalry was not moral principle or love of justice and right; it was mere punctiliousness in respect to certain conventional forms.

Immediately on the death of the king, orders were sent to all the ports in the southern part of England forbidding any ship or boat of any kind from going to sea. The object of this was to keep the death of the king a secret from the King of France, for fear that he might seize the opportunity for an invasion of England. Indeed, it was known that he was preparing an expedition for this purpose before the king died, and it was considered very important that he should not hear of the event until the government should be settled, lest he should take advantage of it to hasten his invasion.

The making of these arrangements, and the funeral ceremonies connected with the interment of the king, occupied some days. There was also a difficulty between the Duke of Lancaster and the citizens of London to be settled, which for a time threatened to be quite embarrassing. The case was this.

In all accounts of the Reformation in England, among the earliest of those who first called in question the supremacy of the Pope, the name of Wickliffe is always mentioned. Indeed, he has been called the morning star of the English Reformation, as he appeared before it, and, by the light which beamed from his writings and his deeds, announced and ushered its approach. He was a collegian of the great University of Oxford, a very learned man, and a great student of ecclesiastical and civil law. During the reign of Edward, Richard's grandfather, who had now just died, there had been some disputes between him and the Pope in relation to their respective rights and powers within the realm of England. This is not the place to explain the particulars of the dispute. It is enough here to say that there were two parties formed in England, some taking sides with the Church, and others with the king. The bishops and clergy, of course, belonged to the former class, and many of the high nobility to the latter. At length, after various angry discussions, the Pope issued a bull, addressed to the Archbishop of Canterbury and to the Bishop of London, two of the highest ecclesiastical dignitaries of the realm, commanding them to cause Wickliffe to be apprehended and brought before them for trial on the charge of heresy.

The decrees of popes were in those days, as now, generally called bulls. The reason why they were called by this name was on account of their being authenticated by the Pope's seal, which was impressed upon a sort of button or boss of metal attached to the parchment by a cord or ribbon. The Latin name for this boss was *bulla*. Such bosses were sometimes made of lead, so as to be easily stamped by the seal. Sometimes they were made of other metals. There was one famous decree of the Pope in which the boss was of gold. This was called the golden bull.

On the adjoining page we have an engraving, copied from a very ancient book, representing an archbishop reading a bull to the people in a church. You can see the boss of metal, with the seal stamped upon it, hanging down from the parchment.

The Bull

As soon as the Archbishop of Canterbury and the Bishop of London received the bull commanding them to bring Wickliffe to trial, they caused him to be seized and brought to London. On hearing of his arrest, a number of his friends among the nobles came at once to London too, in order that they might support him by their countenance and encouragement, and restrain the prelates from carrying their hostility against him too far. Among these were the Duke of Lancaster and a certain Lord Percy, a nobleman of very high rank and station. The trial took place in the Church of St. Paul's. Wickliffe was called upon to answer to the charges made against him before a very imposing court of ecclesiastics, all dressed magnificently in their sacerdotal robes. The knights and barons who took Wickliffe's side were present too in their military costume, and a great assembly besides, consisting chiefly of the citizens of London.

The common people of London, being greatly under the influence of the priests, were, of course, against Wickliffe, and they looked with evil eyes upon the Duke of Lancaster and the other nobles who had come there to befriend him. In the course of the trial, which it seems was not conducted in a very regular manner, the prelates and the nobles got into a dispute. The dispute at last became so violent that the Duke of Lancaster had the rudeness to threaten the Bishop of London that if he did not behave better he would drag him out of the church by the hair of his head. This was certainly very rough language to address to a bishop, especially at a time when he was sitting, under authority from the Pope, as a judge in a high spiritual court, and clothed in all the paraphernalia of his sacred office. The Londoners were excessively angry. They went out and called their fellow-citizens to arms. The excitement spread and increased during the night, and the next morning a mob collected in the streets, threatening vengeance against the duke and Lord Percy, and declaring that they would kill them. The duke's arms, which were displayed in a public place in the city, they reversed, as was customary in the case of traitors, and then growing more and more excited as they went on, they directed their steps toward the palace of the Savoy, where they expected to find the duke himself. The duke was not there, but the men would have set fire to the palace had it not been for the interposition of the Bishop of London. He, hearing what was going on, repaired to the spot, and with great difficulty succeeded in restraining the mob and saving the palace. They, however, proceeded forthwith to the house of Lord Percy, where they burst through the doors, and, ransacking all the rooms, tore and broke every thing to pieces, and threw the fragments out at the windows. They found a man dressed as a priest, whom they took to be Lord Percy in disguise, and they killed him on the spot.

The murdered man was not Lord Percy, however, but a priest in his own proper dress. Lord Percy and the duke were just preparing to sit down to dinner quietly together in another place, when a messenger came breathless and informed them what was going on. They immediately fled. They ran to the water-side, got into a boat, and rowed themselves over to Kennington, a place on the southern side of the river, nearly opposite to Westminster, where the young Prince Richard and his mother were then residing; for all this took place just before King Richard's grandfather died.

The lord-mayor and aldermen of London were greatly alarmed when they heard of this riot, and of the excesses which the citizens of London had committed. They were afraid that the Duke of Lancaster, whose influence and power they knew was already very great, and which would probably become vastly greater on the death of the king, would hold them responsible for it. So they went in a body to Richmond, where the king was lying sick, and made very humble apologies for the indignities which had been offered to the duke, and they promised to do all in their power to punish the transgressors. The king was, however, too far gone to pay much attention to this embassy. The mayor and aldermen then sent a deputation to Prince Richard at Kennington, to declare their good-will to him, and their readiness to accept him as their sovereign upon the death of his grandfather, and to promise faithful allegiance to him on their own part individually, and on the part of the city of London. They hoped by this means to conciliate the good opinion of Richard and of his mother, as well as of the other friends around him, and prepare them to judge leniently of their case when it should come before them.

All this, as has already been remarked, took place just before King Edward's death. Immediately after his death Richard and his mother went to Richmond, and took up their residence in the palace where Edward died. On the next day a deputation was sent to the mayor and aldermen of London in Richard's name, calling upon them to appear at Richmond before the king, together with the Duke of Lancaster and his friends, in order that both sides might be heard in respect to the subject-matter of the dispute, and that the question might be properly decided. The Duke of Lancaster, they were informed, had agreed to this course, and was ready to appear. They were accordingly summoned to appear also.

The Londoners were at first rather afraid to obey this injunction. They did not think that a boy of eleven years of age was really competent to hear and decide such a case. Then they were afraid, too, that the Duke of Lancaster, being his uncle, would have such an influence over him as to lead him to decide just as he, the duke, should desire, and that thus, if they submitted to such a hearing of the case, they would place themselves wholly in the duke's power. After some hesitation, however, they finally concluded to go, stipulating only that, whatever disposal might be made of the case, there should, in no event, any personal harm befall the mayor or the aldermen.

This condition was agreed to, and the parties appeared on the appointed day before the little king to have the case tried. Richard was, of course, surrounded by his officers and counselors, and the business was really transacted by them, though it was done in the young king's name. There was no difficulty in settling the dispute amicably, for all parties were disposed to have it settled, and in such cases it is always easy to find a way. In this instance, the advisers of Richard managed so well that the duke and his friends were quite reconciled to the Londoners, and they all went out from the presence of the king at last, when the case was concluded, as good friends apparently as they had ever been.

The settling of this dispute was the first act of King Richard's reign. Considering how violent the dispute had been, and how powerful the parties to it were, and also considering that Richard was yet nothing but a small though very pretty boy, we must admit that it was a very good beginning.

7

The Coronation

A.D. 1377

Nature and design of a coronation.—Arrangements made for Richard's coronation.—Conduits of wine.—Golden snow.—The young girls.—Procession.—Crowds of people in the streets.—Ceremonies of the coronation.—Bewildering scene.—Oath administered to the people.—Ceremony of anointing.—Richard clothed in his royal robes.—The crown.—The globe.—The sceptre.—Richard makes his offerings at the altar.—Richard is entirely exhausted with fatigue.—Creation of earls.—Rude amusements.—Wine.—French invasions.—Richard's uncles.—His bright prospects.

THE coronation of a monarch is often postponed for a considerable time after his accession to the throne. There is no practical inconvenience in such a postponement, for the crowning, though usually a very august and imposing ceremony, is of no particular force or effect in respect to the powers or prerogatives of the king. He enters upon the full enjoyment of all these prerogatives and powers at once on the death of his predecessor, and can exercise them all without restraint, as the public good may require. The coronation is merely a pageant, which, as such, may be postponed for a longer or shorter period, as occasion may require.

Richard was crowned, however, a very short time after his father's death. It was thought best, undoubtedly, to take prompt measures for sealing and securing his right to the succession, lest the Duke of Lancaster or some other person might be secretly forming plans to supplant him. King Edward, Richard's grandfather, died on the 22d of June. The funeral occupied several days, and immediately afterward arrangements began to be made for the coronation. The day was appointed for the 16th of July. On the 15th the king was to proceed in state from the palace in the environs of London where he had been residing, through the city of London, to Westminster, where the coronation was to take place; and as the people of London desired to make a grand parade in honor of the passage of the king through the city, the arrangements of the occasion comprised two celebrations on two successive days— the procession through London on the 15th, and the coronation at Westminster on the 16th.

On the morning of the 15th, an imposing train of the nobility, led by all the great officers of state, assembled at the residence of the king to receive him and to escort him through the city. Richard was dressed in magnificent robes, and mounted upon a handsome charger. A nobleman led his horse by the bridle. Another nobleman of high rank went before him, bearing the sword of state, the emblem of the regal power. Other nobles and prelates in great numbers, mounted many of them on splendidly-caparisoned horses, and in full armor, joined in the train. Bands of musicians, with trumpets and other martial instruments in great numbers, filled the air with joyful sounds, and in this manner the procession commenced its march.

In the meantime, the Londoners had made great preparations for the reception of the *cortège*. Conduits were opened in various parts of the city, to run with wine instead of water, in token of the general joy. In the heart of the city an edifice in the form of a castle was erected in honor of the occasion. This castle had four towers. In each of the towers were four beautiful young girls, all about Richard's age. They were dressed in white, and their duty was, as the king went by, to throw out a quantity of little leaves of gold, which, falling upon and all around the king, produced the effect of a shower of golden flakes of snow.

The procession stopped before the castle. There were conduits flowing with wine upon two sides of it. The young girls descended from the towers, bringing golden cups in their hands. These cups they filled with wine at the fountains, and offered them to the king and to the nobles who accompanied him. On the top of the castle, between the four towers, there stood a golden angel with a crown in his hand. By some ingenious mechanism, this angel was made to extend his arm to the king, as if in the act of offering him the crown. This was a symbol representing the idea often inculcated in those days, that the right of the king to reign was a divine right, as if the crown were placed upon his head by an angel from heaven.

After pausing thus a short time at the castle, the procession moved on. The streets were filled with vast crowds of people, who drowned the music of the trumpets and drums by their continual acclamations.

In this way the royal procession passed on through London, and at length arrived at the gate of the palace in Westminster. Here Richard was assisted to dismount from his horse, and was conducted into the palace between two long lines of knights and soldiers that were stationed at the entrance and upon the staircase to honor his arrival. He was glad that the ceremony was over, for he was beginning to be very tired of riding on horseback so many hours, and of being so long in the midst of scenes of so much noise, excitement, and confusion.

The next day was the day appointed for the coronation itself. Richard was dressed in his royal robes, and shortly before noon he was conducted in great state from the palace to the church. He was received by a procession of bishops and monks, and conducted by them to the grand altar. The pavement before the altar was covered with rich tapestry. Here Richard kneeled while prayers were said and the Litany was sung by the priests. His barons and nobles, and the great officers of state, kneeled around him. After the prayers were over, he was conducted to an elevated seat, which was richly decorated with carvings and gold.

A bishop then ascended to a pulpit built against one of the vast Gothic columns of the church, and preached a sermon. The sermon was on the subject of the duty of a king; explaining how a king ought to conduct himself in the government of his people, and enjoining upon the people, too, the duty of being faithful and obedient to their king.

Richard paid little attention to this sermon, being already tired of the scene. He was, moreover, bewildered by the multitude of people crowded into the church, and all gazing intently and continually upon him. There were bishops and priests in their sacerdotal robes of crimson and gold, and knights and nobles brilliant with nodding plumes and glittering armor of steel. When the sermon was finished, the oath was administered to Richard. It was read by the archbishop, Richard assenting to it when it was read. As soon as the oath had thus been administered, the archbishop, turning in succession to each quarter of the church, repeated the oath in a loud voice to the people, four times in all, and called upon those whom he successively addressed to ask whether they would submit to Richard as their king. The people on each side, as he thus addressed them in turn, answered, with a loud voice, that they would obey him. This ceremony being ended, the archbishop turned again toward Richard, pronounced certain additional prayers, and then gave him his benediction.

The ceremony of anointing came next. The archbishop advanced to Richard and began to take off the robes in which he was attired. At the same time, four earls held over and around him, as a sort of screen, a coverture, as it was called, of cloth of gold. Richard remained under this coverture while he was anointed. The archbishop took off nearly all his clothes, and then anointed him with the holy oil. He applied the oil to his head, his breast, his shoulders, and the joints of his arms, repeating, as he did so, certain prayers. The choir, in the meantime, chanted a portion of the Scriptures relating to the anointing of King Solomon. When the oil had been applied, the archbishop put upon the king a long robe, and directed him to kneel. Richard accordingly kneeled again upon the tapestry which covered the floor, the archbishop and the bishops kneeling around him. While in this position the archbishop offered more prayers, and more hymns were sung, and then he assisted Richard to rise from his kneeling posture, and proceeded to dress and equip him with the various garments, and arms, and emblems appropriate to the kingly power. In putting on each separate article the archbishop made a speech in Latin, according to a form provided for such occasions, beginning with, Receive this cloak, receive this stole, receive this sword, and the like. [The stole was a long narrow scarf, fringed at the ends. It was wound about the neck and crossed over the breast, and was worn as a badge.]

In this manner and with these ceremonies Richard was invested with a splendidly-embroidered coat and cloak, a stole, a sword, a pair of spurs, a pair of bracelets, and, finally, with a garment over all called the pallium. All these things, of course, had been made expressly for the occasion, and were adapted to the size and shape of a boy like Richard. The archbishop was assisted in putting these things on by certain nobles of the court, who had been designated for this purpose, and who considered themselves highly honored by the part that was assigned them in the ceremony.

When the dressing had been completed, the archbishop took the crown, and after having invoked a blessing upon it by his prayers and benedictions, all in the Latin tongue, he placed it upon Richard's head, repeating, at the same time, a Latin form, the meaning of which was that he received the crown from God Almighty, and that to God alone he was responsible for the exercise of his royal power.

Then came a certain grand officer of the court with a red globe, an emblem of royalty which has long been used in England. This globe the archbishop blessed, and then the officer put it into Richard's hands. In the same manner the sceptre was brought, and, after being blessed by means of the same ceremonies and prayers, was also put into Richard's hands.

Richard was now completely invested with the badges and insignia of his office. The archbishop then, raising his hands, pronounced upon him his apostolic benediction, and the ceremony, so far, was ended. The bishops and nobles then came up to congratulate and salute Richard on having thus received his crown, after which they conducted him to his seat again.

Richard now began to be very tired and to wish to go home, but there was a great deal more yet to come before he could be set at liberty. There was an anthem to be sung by the choir, and more prayers to be said, after which there came what was called the offertory. This was a ceremony in which a person was led to the altar, to lay down upon it whatever offering he chose to make for the service of the Church. The king rose from his seat and was led forward to the altar, having, of course, been previously told what he was to do. He had in his hand a sum of money which had been provided for the occasion. He laid down this money first upon the altar, and then his sword. It was the custom in these coronations for the king thus to offer his sword, in token of the subordination of his royal power to the law and will of God, and then the sword was afterward to be redeemed with money by the sword-bearer, the officer whose duty it was, on leaving the church, to bear the sword in procession before the king.

Accordingly, after Richard had returned from the altar, the earl whose office it was to bear the sword went to the altar and redeemed it with a sum of money, and carried it back to the place where Richard was sitting.

Then came the service of the mass, which occupied a long time, so that Richard became very tired indeed before it was ended. After the mass came the communion, which it was necessary for Richard to partake. The communion was, of course, accompanied with more prayers and more chantings, until the poor boy thought that the ceremonies would never be ended. When at last, however, all was over, and the procession was ready to form again to leave the church, Richard was so worn out and exhausted with the fatigue that he had endured that he could not ride home; so they brought a sort of litter and placed him upon it, and four of the knights bore him home on their shoulders.

His uncle the Duke of Lancaster and the Earl Percy went before him, and a long train of bishops, nobles, and grand officers of state followed behind. In this way he was brought back to the palace. As soon as the party reached the palace, they carried Richard directly up to a chamber, took off all his grand paraphernalia, and put him to bed.

He rested a little while, and then they brought him something to eat. His troubles were, however, not yet over, for there was to be a great banquet that afternoon and evening in the hall of the palace, and it was necessary that he should be there. Accordingly, after a short time, he was arrayed again in his royal robes and insignia, and conducted down to the hall. Here he had a ceremony to perform of creating certain persons earls. Of course it was his counselors that decided who the persons were that were to be thus raised to the peerage, and they told him also exactly what he was to do and say in the programme of the ceremony. He sat upon his throne, surrounded by his nobles and officers of state, and did what they told him to do. When this ceremony had been performed, the whole company sat down to the tables which had been prepared for a banquet.

They continued their feasting and carousing to a late hour, and then amused themselves with various boisterous games common in those days. In the court-yard of the palace a pillar was set up, with pipes at the sides of it, from which there were flowing continually streams of wine of different kinds, and everybody who pleased was permitted to come and drink. A part of the amusement consisted in the pushings and strugglings of the people to get to the faucets, and the spilling of the wine all over their faces and clothes. The top of the pillar was adorned with a large gilt image of an eagle.

The next day there were more processions and more celebrations, but Richard himself was, fortunately for him, excused from taking any part in them. In the meantime, the people who managed the government in Richard's name heard the news that the French had learned, in some way, the tidings of King Edward's death, and had landed in the southern part of England, and were burning and destroying all before them. So they made all haste to raise an army to go and repel the invaders.

It was finally concluded, also, to appoint Richard's two uncles, namely, John, Duke of Lancaster, and Edmund, Earl of Cambridge, as his guardians until he should become of age. Some persons thought it was not safe to trust Richard to the Duke of Lancaster at all, but others thought it would be better to conciliate him by treating him with respect, than to make him an open enemy by passing over him entirely.

Richard was considered, at this time, a very amiable and good boy, and it was generally believed by the people of England that, with a right and proper training, he would grow up to be a virtuous and honest man, and they anticipated for him a long and happy reign. And yet, in a little more than ten years after he became of age, he was disgraced and dethroned on account of his vices and crimes.

8

Chivalry

A.D. 1378-1380

Edmund, Earl of Cambridge.—Thomas of Woodstock.—Richard's young cousin, Henry of Bolingbroke.—A boy king in France.—Richard and Henry Bolingbroke.—French incursions into the Isle of Wight.—Curious story of the Scotch borderers.—Their strange ideas of the grace of God.—Nature of the royal government.—The House of Commons.—Luxury and extravagance of the nobility.—Wars.—Modes of warfare.—Mining.—Besieging engines.—The Duke of Lancaster's sow.—Gunpowder.—Story of the Welsh knight, Evan.—Siege of Mortain.—Situation of the castle.—Evan's hostility to the English.—Hatred of the English against Evan.—John Lamb.—John Lamb arrives at Mortain.—His reception by Evan.—State of the siege.—Curious manners and customs.—John Lamb accomplishes his purpose.—Death of Evan.—Interview between John Lamb and the governor of the castle.—The knights loved fighting for its own sake.—Their love of glory.—Story of De Langurant.—His men.—He challenges the governor of the castle to single combat.—Encounter of the knights.—Use of lances.—Manner in which such combats were fought.—Result of the combat between De Langurant and Bernard.—De Langurant refuses to surrender.—His fate.—Intolerable tyranny of the nobles in those days.—Oppression of the tax-gatherers.— Richard's helplessness.

BESIDES his uncle John, Duke of Lancaster, Richard had two other uncles, who each acted an important part in public affairs at the commencement of his reign. They were,

1. His uncle Edmund, who was the Earl of Cambridge, and afterward Duke of York. Of course he is sometimes called, in the histories of those times, by one of these names, and sometimes by the other.

2. His uncle Thomas. Thomas was born in the palace of Woodstock, and so was often called Thomas of Woodstock. He was the Earl of Buckingham, and afterward the Duke of Gloucester.

Besides these uncles, Richard had a cousin just about his own age, who afterward, as we shall see, played a very important part indeed in Richard's history. This cousin was named Henry Bolingbroke. He was the son of Richard's uncle John, the Duke of Lancaster. He and Richard were now both about eleven years of age; or rather, Richard was eleven, and his cousin Henry was about ten.

Of course, Richard was altogether too young to exercise any real control in respect to the government of the country. Everything was, consequently, left to the Parliament and the nobles. His uncles endeavored to assume the general direction of affairs, but there was nevertheless a strong party against them. There were no means of deciding these disputes except by the votes in Parliament, and these votes went one way and the other, as one party or the other, for the time being, gained the ascendency. Everyone watched very closely the conduct of Richard's uncle John. He was the next oldest son of Edward the Third, after Edward, the Prince of Wales, Richard's father. Of course, if Richard were to die, he would become king; and if he himself were to die before Richard did, and then Richard were to die before he grew up and had children of his own, then his son, Richard's cousin, Henry Bolingbroke, would be entitled to claim the kingdom. Thus, while Richard remained

THE HISTORY OF RICHARD THE SECOND

unmarried and without heirs, this Henry Bolingbroke was in the direct line of succession, and, of course, next to Richard himself, he was, perhaps, the most important personage in the kingdom. There was, it is true, another child, the grandchild of an older uncle of Richard's, named Lionel; but he was very young at this time, and he died not long afterward, leaving Henry Bolingbroke the only heir.

It is curious enough that, a year or two after this, the French king died, and was succeeded by his son, a boy of about twelve years of age. This boy was Charles the Sixth. He was crowned in France with ceremonies still more splendid and imposing in some respects than those which had been observed in London on the occasion of Richard's coronation. Thus the hopes and fears of all the millions of people inhabiting France and England respectively, in regard to the succession of the crown and the government of the country, were concentrated in three boys not yet in their teens.

Of course, Richard and his cousin Henry Bolingbroke were rivals from the beginning. Richard and his friends were jealous and suspicious of Henry and of his father, and were always imagining that they were wishing that Richard might die, in order that they might come into his place. Thus there was no cordial friendship in the family, nor could there be any. Of the other nobles and barons, some took sides in one way and some in the other. The boys themselves, both Richard and Henry, were too young to know much about these things; but the leading barons and courtiers formed themselves into parties, ranging themselves some on one side and some on the other, so as to keep up a continual feeling of jealousy and ill-will.

In the meantime, the French began to retaliate for the invasions of their country which the English had made, by planning invasions of England in return. One expedition landed on the Isle of Wight, and after burning and destroying the villages and small towns, they laid some of the large towns under a heavy contribution; that is, they made them pay a large sum of money under a threat that, if the money was not paid, they would burn down their town too. So the citizens collected the money and paid it, and the French expedition set sail and went away before the government had time to send troops from London to intercept them.

The French, too, besides invading England themselves on the south, incited the Scotch to make incursions into the northern provinces, for Scotland was then entirely independent of England. A curious story is related illustrating the religious ignorance which prevailed among the common people of Scotland in those days. It seems that some remarkable epidemic prevailed in 1379 in the northern part of England, which was extremely fatal. Great numbers of people died. The Scotch sent messengers across the border to ascertain what the cause of the sickness was. The English people told them that they did not know what the cause was. It was a judgment from God, the nature and operation of which was hidden from them. They added, however, this pious sentiment, that they submitted themselves patiently to the dispensation, for they knew "that every calamity that could befall men in this world came from the grace of God, to the end that, being punished for their sins, they might be led to repent and reform their wicked lives."

The messengers went home, and reported to the Scottish borderers that the English people said that the plague came from the grace of God, not being able, it would seem, to remember the rest of the message. So the priests arranged a form of prayer, addressed to certain saints, which was to be said by the people every morning. This prayer implored the saints to deliver the people from the grace of God, and the dreadful plagues which were sent by it upon men. The form was this:

> The head of the family would first say,
> "Blessed be," and the others would respond, "The Lord."
>
> Then the head of the family would say,
> "God and Saint Mango,
> Saint Romane and Saint Andro,

Shield us this day from God's grace, and
the foul death that Englishmen die of."

And all the others would say "Amen."

Thus they considered the grace of God as an evil which they were to pray to be delivered from.

Indeed, the common people at this time, not only in Scotland, but throughout England, were in a state of great ignorance and degradation. The barons, and knights, and soldiers generally looked down with great contempt upon all who were engaged in any industrial pursuits. In the country, the great mass of those who were employed in tilling the ground were serfs or slaves, bought and sold with the land, and at the disposal, in almost all respects, of their haughty masters. The inhabitants of the towns, who lived by the manufacturing arts or by commerce, were more independent, but the nobles, and knights, and all who considered themselves gentlemen looked down with something like contempt upon these too, as, in fact, their successors, the present aristocracy of England, do at the present day, regarding them as persons in a very mean condition, and engaged in low and ignoble pursuits. Still, the industrial classes had increased greatly in wealth and numbers, and they began to have and to express some opinion in respect to public affairs. They had considerable influence in the House of Commons; and the government was, in a great measure, dependent upon the House of Commons, and was becoming more and more so every year. It is true, the king, or rather the great lords who managed the government in his name, could make war where they pleased, and appoint whom they pleased to carry it on. Still, they could not assess any tax except by the consent of the Commons, and thus, in carrying on any great operations, they were becoming every year more and more dependent on the public sentiment of the country.

The country began to be very much dissatisfied with the management of public affairs within two or three years after the commencement of Richard's reign. Large sums of money were raised, and put into the hands of Richard's uncles, who spent it in organizing great expeditions by land and sea to fight the French; but almost all of these expeditions were unsuccessful. The people thought that they were mismanaged, and that the money was squandered. Some of the nobles expended immense sums upon themselves. In the case of one expedition that put to sea from the southern coast of England, the nobleman who commanded it had twenty-five vessels loaded with his own personal property and baggage, and that of his servants and attendants. This man had fifty-two new suits of apparel, made of cloth of gold, immensely expensive. The fleet was wrecked, and all this property was lost in the sea.

A great many of the expeditions that were fitted out in England were for the purpose of carrying on wars in Brittany and Aquitaine, in France, for the benefit exclusively of the nobles and knights who claimed possessions in those countries; the mass of the people of England, at whose expense the operations were carried on, having no interest whatever in the result. The worst of it was, that in these wars no real progress was made. Towns were taken and castles were stormed, first by one party and then by the other. The engraving represents the storming of one of these towns, and, being copied from an ancient picture, it shows truthfully the kind of armor and the mode of fighting employed in those days.

Almost the only way of forcing a passage into a castle or fortified town was by climbing over the walls by means of ladders, and overpowering the garrison upon the top of them by main force, as represented in the engraving. Sometimes, it is true, the besiegers of a castle undermined the walls, so as to make them fall in and thus open a breach. At the present day, mines dug in this way are blown up by gunpowder. But people were little acquainted with the use of gunpowder then, and so they were obliged to shore up the walls while they were digging them by means of posts and beams, and these, after the miners had withdrawn, were pulled out by ropes, and thus the walls were made to fall down.

THE HISTORY OF RICHARD THE SECOND

The Storming of a Town

Great engines were sometimes used, too, to batter down the walls of castles and towns. There was one kind of engine, used by the Duke of Lancaster in one of his campaigns in France in the early part of Richard's reign, which was called a *sow*. The sow was made in many parts, at a distance from the place besieged, wherever a suitable supply of beams and timber could be obtained, and then was brought on carts to the spot. When it was framed together and put in operation, it would hurl immense stones, which, striking the walls, made breaches in them, or, going over them, came down into the interior of the place, crushing through the roofs of the houses, and killing sometimes multitudes of men. The sow was made, too, so as to afford shelter and protection to a great number of persons, who could ride upon it while it was drawn or pushed up near the walls, and thus reach a point where they could begin to undermine the walls, or plant their ladders for scaling them. The Duke of Lancaster caused one sow to be made which would carry, in this way, one hundred men.

Gunpowder, however, began to be used about this time, though in a very imperfect and inefficient manner. At one siege, namely, that of St. Malo, a town on the northwestern coast of France, it is said that the

Duke of Lancaster had four hundred cannon. They were all, however, of very little avail in taking the town.

The wars waged between the English and the French in these chivalrous times were much more personal in their character than wars are at the present day. In that period of the world, every great duke, or baron, or knight was in some sense an independent personage, having his own separate interests to look out for, and his own individual rights and honor to maintain, to a degree far greater than now. The consequence of this was, that the narratives of wars of those times contain accounts of a great many personal incidents and adventures which make the history of them much more entertaining than the histories of modern campaigns. I will give one or two examples of these personal incidents.

At one time, while the Duke of Lancaster was besieging St. Malo with his four hundred cannon, there was a famous Welsh knight, named Evan, known in history as Evan of Wales, who was besieging a castle belonging to the English. The name of the castle was Mortain. It was on the River Garonne, in the country of Aquitaine. The castle was so strong that Evan had no hope of taking it by force, and so he invested it closely on all sides, and sat down quietly waiting for the garrison to be starved into a surrender.

The castle was near the river. Evan built three block-houses on the three sides of it. One of these block-houses was on the edge of a rock before the castle, on the river side. The second was opposite a postern gate, and was intended particularly to watch the gate, in order to prevent any one from coming out or going in. The third block-house was below the castle, between the lower part of it and the water. To guard the fourth side of the castle, Evan had taken possession of a church which stood at some little distance from it, and had converted the church into a fort. Thus the castle was completely invested, being watched and guarded on every side. The garrison, however, would not surrender, hoping that they might receive succor before their provisions were entirely exhausted. They remained in this condition for a year and a half, and were at length reduced to great distress and suffering. Still, the governor of the castle would not surrender.

It may seem strange that Evan, a knight from Wales, should be fighting against the English, since Wales had some years before been annexed to the realm of England. The reason was, that Evan's family had been driven out of Wales by the cruelties and oppressions of the English. His father, who had formerly been Prince of Wales, had been beheaded, and Evan, in his infancy, had been saved by his attendants, who fled with him to France. There he had been received into the family of the French king, John, and, after he had grown up, he had fought under John many years. The older he grew, the more his heart was filled with resentment against the English, and now he was engaged, heart and hand, in the attempt to drive them out of France. Of course, the English considered him a traitor, and they hated him much more than they did any of the French commanders, of whom nothing else was to be expected than that they should be enemies to the English, and fight them always and every where. Evan they considered as in some sense one of their own countrymen who had turned against them.

There was another circumstance which increased the hatred of the English against Evan, and that was, that he had taken one of their knights prisoner, and then refused to ransom him on any terms. The English offered any sum of money that Evan would demand, or they offered to exchange for him a French knight of the same rank; but Evan was inexorable. He would not give up his prisoner on any terms, but sent him to Paris, and shut him up in a dungeon, where he pined away, and at length died of misery and despair.

In consequence of these things, a plot was formed in England for assassinating Evan. A Welshman, by the name of John Lamb, was appointed to execute it.

John Lamb set out from England, and crossed the Channel to France. He was a well-educated man, speaking French fluently, and he was well received every where by the French, for he told them that he was a countryman of Evan's, and that he was going to Mortain to join him. The French, accordingly, treated him well, and helped him forward on his journey.

When he reached Mortain, he came into the presence of Evan, and, falling on his knees before him, he said that he was his countryman, and that he had come all the way from Wales to enter into his service. Evan did not suspect any treachery. He received the man kindly, and made many inquiries of him in respect to the news which he brought from Wales.

John gave him very favorable accounts of the country, and spoke particularly of the interest and affection which was every where felt for him.

"The whole country," said he, "are thinking and talking continually about you, and are anxiously desiring your return. They wish to have you for their lord."

These and other flatteries quite won the heart of Evan, and he took Lamb into his service, and appointed him to a confidential post about his person.

For a time after this there were occasional skirmishes between the garrison of Mortain and the besiegers, but, as the strength of the garrison gradually failed, these contests became less and less frequent, until at last they ceased entirely. The soldiers of Evan then had nothing to do but to watch and wait until the progress of starvation and misery should compel the garrison to surrender. There was no longer any danger of sorties from the walls, and the besiegers ceased to be at all on their guard, but went and came at their ease about the castle, just as if there were no enemy near.

Evan himself used to go out in the morning, when the weather was fine, into the fields in front of the castle before he was dressed, and there have his hair combed and plaited a long time; for, like most of the knights and gentlemen soldiers of those days, he was very particular about his dress and his personal appearance. On these occasions he often had nobody to attend him but John Lamb. There was a place where there was a fallen tree, which formed a good seat, at a spot which afforded a commanding view of the castle and of the surrounding country. He used often to go and sit upon this tree while his hair was combed, amusing himself the while in watching to see what was going on in the castle, and to observe if there were any signs that the garrison were going to surrender.

One morning, after a very warm night, during which Evan had not been able to sleep, he went out to this place very early. He was not dressed, but wore only a jacket and shirt, with a cloak thrown over his shoulders. The soldiers generally were asleep, and there was nobody with Evan but John Lamb. Evan sat down upon the log, and presently sent John Lamb to the block-house for his comb.

"Go and get my comb," said he, "and comb my hair. That will refresh me a little."

So John went for the comb. As he went, however, it seemed to him that the time for the execution of his plan had come. So he brought with him from the block-house a Spanish dagger, which he found there in Evan's apartment. As soon as he reached Evan, who had thrown off his cloak, and was thus almost naked and entirely off his guard, he plunged the dagger into him up to the hilt at a single blow. Evan sank down upon the ground a lifeless corpse. Lamb left the dagger in the wound, and walked directly to the gate of the castle.

The guards at the gate hailed him and demanded what he wanted. He said he wished to see the governor of the castle. So the guards took him in, and conducted him into the presence of the governor.

"My lord," said Lamb, "I have delivered you from one of the greatest enemies you ever had."

"From whom?" asked the governor.

"From Evan of Wales," said Lamb.

The governor was very much astonished at hearing this, and demanded of Lamb by what means he had delivered them from Evan. Lamb then related to the governor what he had done.

The first impression produced upon the governor's mind by the statement which Lamb made was a feeling of displeasure. He looked at the assassin with a scowl of anger upon his face, and said sternly,

"Wretch! you have murdered your master. You deserve to have your head cut off for such a deed; and, were it not that we are in such great straits, and that we gain such very great advantage by his death, I would have your head cut off on the spot. However, what is done can not be undone. Let it pass."

The garrison did not derive any immediate advantage, after all, from the death of Evan, for the French were so incensed by the deed which John Lamb had perpetrated that they sent more troops to the spot, and pressed the siege more closely than ever. The garrison was, however, not long afterward relieved by an English fleet, which came up the river and drove the French away.

The knights and barons of those days were not accustomed to consider it any hardship to go to war against each other, but rather a pleasure. They enjoyed fighting each other just as men at the present day enjoy hunting wild beasts in the forest; and that chieftain was regarded as the greatest and most glorious who could procure for his retainers the greatest amount of this sort of pleasure, provided always that his abilities as a leader were such that they could have their full share of victory in the contests that ensued. It was only the quiet and industrial population at home, the merchants of London, the manufacturers of the country towns, and the tillers of the land, who were impoverished and oppressed by the taxes necessary for raising the money which was required, that were disposed to complain. The knights and soldiers who went forth on these campaigns liked to go. They not only liked the excitements and the freedom of the wild life they led in camp, and of the marches which they made across the country, but they liked the fighting itself. Their hearts were filled with animosity and hatred against their foes, and they were at any time perfectly willing to risk their lives for the opportunity of gratifying these passions. They were also greatly influenced by a love for the praise and glory which they acquired by the performance of any great or brilliant feat of arms.

This led them often to engage in single personal combats, such, for example, as this. There was a certain French knight, named De Langurant: he was making an incursion into the English territories in the neighborhood of Bordeaux. One day he was scouring the country at the head of about forty troopers, armed with lances. At the head of this troop he came into the neighborhood of a village which was in the hands of the English, and was defended by an English garrison. When he approached the village he halted his men, and posted them in ambush in a wood.

"You are to remain here a while," said he. "I am going on alone before the town, to see if I can not find some body to come out to fight me in single combat."

The object of De Langurant in this plan was to show his daring, and to perform a brave exploit which he might have to boast of, and glory over afterward among his brother soldiers.

The men did as he had commanded them, and concealed themselves in the wood. De Langurant then rode on alone, his lance fixed in its rest, and his helmet glittering in the sun, until he reached the gate of the town. Then he halted and challenged the sentinel.

The sentinel demanded what he wanted.

"Where is the captain of this garrison?" said the trooper. "I wish you to go and find him, and tell him that Lord De Langurant is at the gates of the town, and wishes to have a tilt with him. I dare him to come and fight with me, since he pretends that he is such a valiant man. Tell him that if he does not come, I will proclaim him every where as a coward that did not dare to come out and meet me."

The name of the captain whom De Langurant thus challenged was Bernard Courant. It happened that one of Bernard's servants was upon the gate, near the sentinel, at the time this challenge was given. He immediately called out to De Langurant, saying,

"I have heard what you have said, Sir Knight, and I will go immediately and inform my master. You may rely upon seeing him in a few minutes, if you will wait, for he is no coward."

Bernard was greatly incensed when he heard the impertinent and boasting message which De Langurant had sent him. He started up immediately and called for his arms, commanding, at the same time, that his horse should be saddled. He was very soon equipped and ready. The gate was opened, the drawbridge let down, and he sallied forth. De Langurant was waiting for him on the plain.

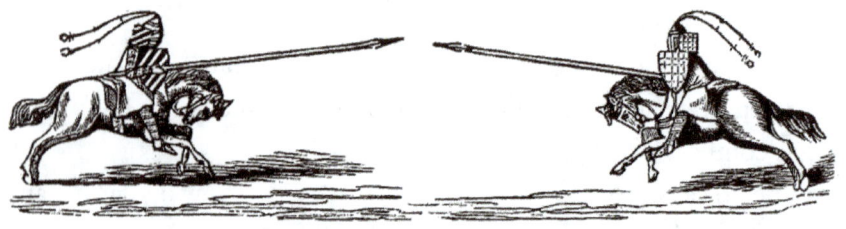

Knights Charging Upon Each Other

This engraving represents the manner in which knights rode to the encounter of each other in single combat. They are each well protected with a helmet, a shield or buckler, and other armor of iron, and are provided with lances and other weapons. These lances were very long, and were made of the toughest wood that could be obtained. The object of each combatant in such an encounter is to strike his antagonist with the point of his weapon so as either to pierce his armor and kill him, or else to throw him off his horse by the shock and force of the blow.

If a knight were unhorsed, he lay generally helpless on the ground, being unable to rise on account of the weight of his armor. Of course, in this situation he was easily vanquished by his adversary.

The knights were both mounted on furious chargers; and, after a moment's pause, during which they eyed each other with looks of fierce defiance, they put spurs to their horses, and the horses began to gallop toward each other at the top of their speed. Each of the knights, as he advanced, had one end of his lance supported in its rest, while he pointed the other directly toward his antagonist, with a view of striking him with it as he rode by, watching, at the same time, the terrible point which was coming toward him, in hopes to avoid it if possible, and, if not, to bear up against the blow so firmly as not to be unhorsed. The lances were very long, and were made of very solid wood, but the chief momentum of the blow which they were intended to give came from the end of them being supported in a rest, which was connected with the saddle in such a manner that the whole impetus of the horse, as it were, was communicated to the lance, and this impetus was so great, that if a lance struck in such a manner that it could not glance off, and did not overthrow the man, but met with a solid resistance, it was often shivered to atoms by the shock. This happened in the present case. The lances of both combatants were shivered at the first encounter. The riders were, however, uninjured. The horses wheeled, made a short circuit, and rushed toward each other again. At the second encounter, Bernard brought down so heavy a blow with a battle-axe upon the iron armor that covered De Langurant's shoulder, that the unfortunate trooper was hurled out of his saddle and thrown to the ground.

As soon as Bernard could rein in his horse again and bring him round, he galloped up to the spot where De Langurant had fallen, and found him attempting to raise himself up from the ground. At the same time, the horsemen whom De Langurant had left in the wood, and who had been watching the combat from their place of ambush, seeing their master unhorsed, began to put themselves in motion to come to his rescue. Bernard, who was a man of prodigious strength, reached down from his horse as he rode over his fallen enemy, and seized hold of his helmet. His horse, in the mean time, going on, and Bernard holding to the helmet with all his force, it was torn off from its fastenings, and De Langurant's head was left unprotected and bare.

Bernard threw the helmet down upon the ground under his horse's feet. Then drawing his dagger, he raised it over De Langurant's head, and called upon him to surrender.

"Surrender!" said he. "Surrender this instant, or you are a dead man."

The men in ambush were coming on, and De Langurant hoped they would be able to rescue him, so he did not reply. Bernard, knowing that he had not a moment to spare, drove the dagger into De Langurant's head, and then galloped away back through the gates into the town, just in time to avoid the troop of horsemen from the ambush, who were bearing down at full speed toward the spot, and were now just at hand.

The gates of the town were closed, and the drawbridge was taken up the moment that Bernard had entered, so that he could not be pursued. The horsemen, therefore, had nothing to do but to bear away their wounded commander to the nearest castle which was in their possession. The next day he died.

* * *

While the barons and knights were thus amusing themselves at the beginning of Richard's reign with fighting for castles and provinces, either for the pleasure of fighting, or for the sake of the renown or the plunder which they acquired when they were fortunate enough to gain the victory, the great mass of the people of England were taxed and oppressed by their haughty masters to an extent almost incredible. The higher nobles were absolutely above all law. One of them, who was going to set off on a naval expedition into France, seized, in the English sea-port which he was leaving, a number of women, the wives and daughters of the citizens, and took them on board his ship, to be at the disposal there of himself and his fellow grandees. For this intolerable injury the husbands and fathers had absolutely no remedy. To crown the wickedness of this deed, when, soon after the fleet had left the port, a storm arose, and the women were terrified at the danger they were in, and their fright, added to the distress they felt at being thus torn away from their families and homes, made them completely and uncontrollably wretched, the merciless nobles threw them overboard to stop their cries.

Taxes were assessed, too, at this time, upon all the people of the kingdom, that were of an extremely onerous character. These taxes were *farmed*, as the phrase is; that is, the right to collect them was sold to contractors, called farmers of the revenue, who paid a certain sum outright to the government, and then were entitled to all that they could collect of the tax. Thus there was no supervision over them in their exactions, for the government, being already paid, cared for nothing more. The consequence was, that the tax-gatherers, who were employed by the contractors, treated the people in the most oppressive and extortionate manner. If the people made complaints, the government would not listen to them, for fear that if they interfered with the tax-gatherers in collecting the taxes, the farmers would not pay so much the next time.

Richard himself, of course, knew nothing about all these things, or, if he did know of them, he was wholly unable to do any thing to prevent them. He was completely in the power of his uncles, and of the other great nobles of the time. The public discontent, however, grew at last so great that there was nothing wanted but a spark to cause it to break out into a flame. There was such a spark furnished at length by an atrocious insult and injury offered to a young girl, the daughter of a tiler, by one of the tax-gatherers. This led to a formidable insurrection, known in history as Wat Tyler's insurrection. I shall relate the story of this insurrection in the next chapter.

9

Wat Tyler's Insurrection

A.D. 1381

Real name of Wat Tyler.—State of the country.—Names of Walter's confederates.—Character of these men.—Condition of the lower classes at this time.—Ball's proposal.—Other orators.—Their discourses.—Mixture of truth and error in their complaints.—Necessary inequality among men.—The true doctrine of equality.—Origin of Wat Tyler's insurrection.—The tax-gatherer in Walter's family.—Intolerable outrage.—The tax-gatherer killed.—Plan of the insurgents to march to London.—Re-enforcements by the way.—Oaths administered.—The Archbishop of Canterbury.—Case of Sir John Newton.—Sir John Newton is sent as an embassador to the king.—Interview between Sir John and the king at the Tower.—Sir John returns to the insurgents.—The king goes down to meet the insurgents.—Scene on the bank of the river.—Parley with the insurgents.—The king retires.—The insurgents resolve to go into London.—The bridge.—Excitement in the city.—The gates opened.—The insurgents occupy the streets of London.—Destruction of the Duke of Lancaster's palace.—Destruction of the Temple.—Assassination of Richard Lyon.—Excesses of the mob.—They bivouac near the Tower.

THE insurrection to which a large portion of the people of England were driven by the cruel tyranny and oppression which they suffered in the early part of King Richard's reign is commonly called Wat Tyler's insurrection, as if the affair with Wat Tyler were the cause and moving spring of it, whereas it was, in fact, only an incident of it.

The real name of this unhappy man was John Walter. He was a tiler by trade—that is, his business was to lay tiles for the roofs of houses, according to the custom of roofing prevailing in those days. So he was called John Walter, the Tiler, or simply Walter the Tiler; and from this his name was abridged to Wat Tyler.

The whole country was in a state of great discontent and excitement on account of the oppressions which the people suffered before Walter appeared upon the stage at all. When at length the outbreak occurred, he came forward as one of the chief leaders of it; there were however, several other leaders. The names by which the principal of them were known were Jack Straw, William Wraw, Jack Shepherd, John Milner, Hob Carter, and John Ball. It is supposed that many of these names were fictitious, and that the men adopted them partly to conceal their real names, and partly because they supposed that they should ingratiate themselves more fully with the lower classes of the people by assuming these familiar and humble appellations.

The historians of the times say that these leaders were all very bad men. They may have been so, though the testimony of the historians is not conclusive on this point, for they belonged to, and wrote in the interest of the upper classes, their enemies. The poor insurgents themselves never had the opportunity to tell their own story, either in respect to themselves or their commanders.

Still, it is highly probable that they were bad men. It is not generally the amiable, the gentle, and the good that are first to rise, and foremost to take the lead in revolts against tyrants and oppressors. It is, on the other hand, far more commonly the violent, the desperate, and the bad that are first goaded on to assume this terrible responsibility. It is, indeed, one of the darkest features of tyranny that it tends, by the reaction which follows it, to invest this class of men with great power, and to commit the best interests of society, and the lives of great numbers of men, for a time at least, entirely to the disposal of the most reckless and desperate characters.

The lower classes of the people of England had been held substantially as slaves by the nobles and gentry for many generations. They had long submitted to this, hopeless of any change. But they had gradually become enlightened in respect to their natural rights; and now, when the class immediately above them were so grievously oppressed and harassed by the taxes which were assessed upon them, and still more by the vexatious and extortionate mode in which the money was collected, they all began to make common cause, and, when the rebellion broke out, they rose in one mass, freemen and bondmen together.

There was a certain priest named John Ball, who, before the rebellion broke out, had done much to enlighten the people as to their rights, and had attempted to induce them to seek redress at first in a peaceable manner. He used to make speeches to the people in the market-place, representing to them the hardships which they endured by the oppressions of the nobility, and urging them to combine together to petition the king for a redress of their grievances. "The king will listen to us, I am sure," said he, "if we go to him together in a body and make our request; but if he will not hear us, then we must redress our grievances ourselves the best way we can."

The example of Ball was followed by many other persons; and, as always happens in such cases, the excitement among the people, and their eagerness to hear, brought out a great many spectators, whose only object was to see who could awaken the resentment and anger of their audiences in the highest degree, and produce the greatest possible excitement. These orators, having begun with condemning the extravagant wealth, the haughty pretensions, and the cruel oppressions of the nobles, and contrasting them with the extreme misery and want of the common people, whom they held as slaves, proceeded at length to denounce all inequalities in human condition, and to demand that all things should be held in common.

"Things will never go on well in England," said they, "until all these distinctions shall be leveled, and the time shall come when there shall be neither vassal nor lord, and these proud nobles shall be no more masters than ourselves. How ill have they used us! And what right have they to hold us in this miserable bondage? Are we not all descended from the same parents, Adam and Eve? What right have one set of men to make another set their slaves? What right have they to compel us to toil all our lives to earn money, that they may live at ease and spend it? They are clothed in velvets and rich stuffs, ornamented with ermine and furs, while we are half naked, or clothed only in rags. They have wines, and spices, and fine bread, while we have nothing but rye, and the refuse of the straw. They have manors and handsome seats, while we live in miserable cabins, and have to brave the wind and rain at our labor in the fields, in order that, with the proceeds of our toil, they may support their pomp and luxury. And if we do not perform our services, or if they unjustly think that we do not, we are beaten, and there is no one to whom we can complain or look for justice."

There is obviously some truth and some extravagance in these complaints. Men deprived of their rights, as these poor English serfs were, and goaded by the oppressions which they suffered almost to despair, will, of course, be extravagant in their complaints. None but those totally ignorant of human nature would expect men to be moderate and reasonable when in such a condition, and in such a state of mind.

The truth is, that there always has been, and there always will necessarily be, a great inequality in the conditions, and a great difference in the employments of men; but this fact awakens no dissatisfaction or discontent when those who have the lower stations of life to fill are treated as they ought to be treated. If they enjoy personal liberty, and are paid the fair wages which they earn by their labor, and are treated with kindness and consideration by those whose duties are of a higher and more intellectual character, and whose position in life is superior to theirs, they are, almost without exception, satisfied and happy. It is only when they are urged and driven hard and long by unfeeling oppression that they are ever aroused to rebellion against the order of the social state; and then, as might be expected, they go to extremes, and, if they get the power into their hands, they sweep every thing away, and overwhelm themselves and their superiors in one common destruction.

Young persons sometimes imagine that the American doctrine of the equality of man refers to equality of condition; and even grown persons, who ought to think more clearly and be more reasonable, sometimes refer to the distinctions of rich and poor in this country as falsifying our political theories. But the truth is, that, in our political theory of equality, it is not at all equality of condition, but equality of *rights*, that is claimed for man. All men—the doctrine is simply— have an equal right to life, liberty, and the pursuit of happiness. Even when all are in the full enjoyment of their rights, different men will, of course, attain to very different degrees of advancement in the objects of their desire. Some will be rich and some will be poor; some will be servants and some masters; some will be the employers and some the employed; but, so long as all are equal *in respect to their rights*, none will complain—or, at least, no *classes* will complain. There will, of course, be here and there disappointed and discontented individuals, but their discontent will not spread. It is only by the long-continued and oppressive infringement of the natural rights of large masses of men that the way is prepared for revolts and insurrections.

It was by this process that the way was prepared for the insurrection which I am now to describe. The whole country for fifty miles about London was in a very sullen and angry mood, ready for an outbreak the moment that any incident should occur to put the excitement in motion. This incident was furnished by an occurrence which took place in the family of Walter the Tiler.

It seems that a personal tax had been levied by the government, the amount of which varied with the age of the individual assessed. Children paid so much. Young men and young women paid more. The line between these classes was not clearly defined, or, rather, the tax-gatherers had no means of determining the ages of the young people in a family, if they suspected the parents reported them wrong. In such cases they were often very insolent and rude, and a great many quarrels took place, by which the people were often very much incensed. The tax-gatherer came one day into Walter's house to collect the tax. Walter himself was away, engaged at work tiling a house nearby. The only persons that were at home were his wife and a young daughter just growing to womanhood. The tax-gatherer said that the girl was full-grown, and that they must pay the higher tax for her. Her mother said, "No, she is not full-grown yet; she is only a child." The tax-gatherer then said he would soon find out whether she was a woman or not, and went to her to take hold of her, offering her rudeness and violence of the worst possible character. The poor girl screamed and struggled to get away from him. Her mother ran to the door, and made a great outcry, calling for help. Walter, hearing the cries, seized for a club a heavy implement which he used in tiling, and ran home. As soon as he entered the house, he demanded of the officer, who had now left his daughter and came forward to meet him, what he meant by conducting in so outrageous a manner in his house. The officer replied defiantly, and advanced toward Walter to strike him. Walter parried the stroke, and then, being roused to perfect phrensy by the insult which his daughter had received and the insolence of the tax-gatherer, he brought his club down upon the tax-gatherer's head with such a blow as to break his skull and kill him on the spot. The blow was so violent that the man's brains were scattered all about the floor.

The news of this occurrence spread like wildfire through the town. The people all took Walter's part, and they began to assemble. It seems that a great many of them had had their daughters maltreated in the same way by the tax-gatherers, but had not dared to resist or to complain. They now, however, flocked around the house of Walter, and promised to stand by him to the end. The plan was proposed that they should march to London, and in a body appeal to the king, and call upon him to redress their wrongs.

"He is young," said they, "and he will have pity upon us, and be just to us. Let us go in a body and petition him."

The news of the movement spread to all the neighboring towns, and very soon afterward a vast concourse collected, and commenced their march toward London. They were joined on the road by large companies that came from the villages and towns on the way, until at length Walter and his fellow-leaders found themselves at the head of from sixty to one hundred thousand men.

View of the Tower of London, as seen from the River

The whole country was, of course, thrown into a state of great alarm. The Duke of Lancaster, who was particularly obnoxious to the people, was absent at this time. He was on the frontiers of Scotland. The king was in his palace; but, on hearing tidings of the insurrection, he went to the Tower, which is a strong castle built on the banks of the river, in the lower part of London. A number of the nobles who had most cause to fear the mob went with him, and shut themselves up there. The Princess of Wales, Richard's mother, happened to be at Canterbury at the time, having gone there on a pilgrimage. She immediately set out on her return to London, but she was intercepted on the way by Tyler and his crowd of followers. The crowd gathered around the carriage, and frightened the princess very much indeed, but they did her no harm. After detaining her for some time, they let her pass on. She immediately made the best of her way to the Tower, where she joined her son.

As fast as companies of men came from the villages and towns along the road to join the insurgents, the leaders administered to them an oath. The oath bound them,

1. Always to be faithful and true to King Richard.

2. Never to submit to the reign of any king named John. This was aimed at the Duke of Lancaster, whose name was John, and whom they all specially hated.

3. Always to follow and defend their leaders whenever called upon to do so, and always to be ready to march themselves, and to bring their neighbors with them, at a moment's warning.

4. To demand the abrogation of all the obnoxious taxes, and never to submit again to the collection of them.

In this manner the throngs moved on along the roads leading to London. They became gradually more and more excited and violent as they proceeded. Soon they began to attack the houses of knights, and nobles, and officers of the government which they passed on the way; and many persons, whom they supposed to be their enemies, they killed. At Canterbury they pillaged the palace of the archbishop. The Archbishop of Canterbury, then as now, drew an immense revenue from the state, and lived in great splendor, and they justly conceived that the luxury and ostentation in which he indulged was in some degree the cause of the oppressive taxation that they endured.

They assaulted a castle on the way, and made prisoner of a certain knight named Sir John Newton, whom they found in it, and compelled him to go with them to London. The knight was very unwilling to go with them, and at first seemed determined not to do so; but they disposed of his objections in a very summary manner.

"Sir John," said they, "unless you go with us at once, and in everything do exactly as we order you, you are a dead man."

So Sir John was compelled to go. They took two of his children with them also, to hold as security, they said, for their father's good behavior.

There were other parties of the insurgents who made prisoners in this way of men of rank and family, and compelled them to ride at the head of their respective columns, as if they were leaders in the insurrection.

In this manner the throngs moved on, until at length, approaching the Thames, they arrived at Blackheath and Greenwich, two villages below London, farther down than the Tower, and near the bank of the river. Here they halted, and determined to send an embassage to the king to demand an audience. The embassador that they were to send was the knight, Sir John Newton.

Sir John did not dare to do otherwise than as the insurgents directed. He went to the river, and, taking a boat, he crossed over to the Tower. The guards received him at the gate, and he was conducted into the presence of the king.

He found the king in an apartment with the princess his mother, and with a number of the nobles and officers of his court. They were all in a state of great suspense and anxiety, awaiting tidings. They knew that the whole country was in commotion, but in respect to what they were themselves to do in the emergency they seem to have had no idea.

Sir John was himself one of the officers of the government, and so he was well known to all the courtiers. He fell on his knees as soon as he entered the king's presence, and begged his majesty not to be displeased with him for the message that he was about to deliver.

"I assure your majesty," said he, "that I come not voluntarily, but on compulsion."

The king said to him that he had nothing to fear, and directed him to proceed at once and deliver his message.

The knight then said that the people who had assembled wished to see the king, and he urgently requested that his majesty would come and meet them at Blackheath.

"They wish you to come by yourself alone," said he. "And your majesty need have no fear for your person, for they will not do you the least harm. They have always respected you, and they will continue to respect and honor you as their king. They only wish to tell you some things which they say it is very necessary that your majesty should hear. They have not informed me what it is that they wish to say, since they desire to communicate it themselves directly to your majesty."

The knight concluded by imploring the king to grant his subjects a favorable answer if he could, or at least to allow him to return to them with such a reply as would convince them that he, their messenger, had fairly delivered his message.

"Because," said he, "they hold my children as hostages, and unless I return they will surely put them to death."

The king replied that the knight should have an answer very soon, and he immediately called a council of his courtiers to consider what should be done. There was much difference of opinion, but it was finally concluded to send word to the men that the king would come down the river on the following day to speak with them, and that, if the leaders would come to the bank of the river opposite Blackheath, he would meet them there.

So Sir John Newton left the Tower, and, recrossing the river in his boat, went back to the camp of the insurgents, and reported to the leaders the answer of the king.

They were very much pleased to hear that the king was coming to meet them. The news was soon communicated to all the host, and it gave universal satisfaction. There were sixty thousand men on the ground, it is said, and, of course, they were very insufficiently provided with food, and not at all with shelter. They, however, began to make arrangements to spend the night as well as they could where they were, in anticipation of the interview with the king on the following day.

On the following morning the king attended mass in solemn state in the chapel of the Tower, and then immediately afterward entered his barge, accompanied by a grand train of officers, knights, and barons. The barge, leaving the Tower stairs, was rowed down the river to the place appointed for the interview. About ten thousand of the insurgents had come to the spot, and when they saw the barge coming in sight with the royal party on board, they burst out into such a terrific uproar, with yells, screams, shouts, outcries, and frantic gesticulations, that they seemed to the king and his party like a company of demons. They had Sir John Newton with them. They had brought him down to the bank of the river, because, as they said, if the king were not to come, they should believe that he had imposed upon them in the message which he had brought, and in that case they were going to cut him to pieces on the spot.

The assembly seemed so noisy and furious that the nobles in attendance on the king were afraid to allow him to land. They advised him to remain in the barge, at a little distance from the shore, and to address the people from the deck. The king resolved to do so. So the barge lay floating on the river, the oarsmen taking a few strokes from time to time to recover the ground lost by the drift of the current. The king stood upon the deck of the barge, with his officers around him, and asked the men on the shore what they wished for.

"I have come at your request," said he, "to hear what you have to say."

Such an arrangement as this for communicating with a mass of desperate and furious men would not have been safe under circumstances similar to those of the present day. A man standing in this way on the deck of a boat, within speaking distance of the shore, might, with a rifle, or even with a musket, have been killed in a moment by any one of the thousands on the shore. In those days, however, when the only missiles were spears, javelins, and arrows, a man might stand at his ease within speaking distance of his enemies, entirely out of reach of their weapons.

When the crowd upon the shore saw that the king was waving his hand to them in order to silence them, and that he was trying to speak, they became in some measure calm; and when he asked again what they wished for, the leaders replied by saying that they wished him to come on shore. They desired him to land, they said, so that he could better hear what they had to say.

One of the officers about the king replied that that could not be.

"The king can not land among you," he said. "You are not properly dressed, nor in a fit condition, in any respect, to come into his majesty's presence."

Hereupon the noise and clamor was renewed, and became more violent than ever, the men insisting that the king should land, and filling the air with screams, yells, and vociferations of all sorts, which made the scene truly terrific. The counselors of the king insisted that it was not safe for the king to remain any longer on the river, so the oarsmen were ordered to pull their oars, and the barge immediately began to recede from the shore, and to move back up the river. It happened that the tide was now coming in, and this assisted them very much in their progress, and the barge was swept back rapidly toward the Tower.

The insurgents were now in a great rage. Those who had come down to the bank of the river to meet the king went back in a throng to the place where the great body of the rebels were encamped on the plain. The news that the king had refused to come and hear their complaints was soon spread among the whole multitude, and the cry was raised, To London! To London! So the whole mighty mass began to put itself in motion, and in a few hours all the roads that led toward the metropolis were thronged with vast crowds of ragged and wretched-looking men, barefooted, bareheaded; some bearing rudely-made flags and banners, some armed with clubs and poles, and such other substitutes for weapons as they had been able to seize for the occasion, and all in a state of wild and phrensied excitement.

The people of London were greatly alarmed when they heard that they were coming. There was then but one bridge leading into London from the southern side of the river. This bridge was on the site of the present London Bridge, about half a mile above the Tower. There was a gate at the end of the bridge next the town, and a drawbridge outside of it. The Londoners shut the gate and took up the drawbridge, to prevent the insurgents from coming in.

When the rioters reached the bridge, and found that they were shut out, they, of course, became more violent than before, and they began to burn and destroy the houses outside. Now it happened that many of these houses were handsome villas which belonged to the rich citizens of the town. These citizens became alarmed for their property, and they began to say that it would be better, after all, to open the gates and let the people come in.

"If we let them come in," said they, "they will wander about the streets a while, but they will soon get tired and go away; whereas, by opposing and thwarting them, we only make them the more violent and mischievous."

Then, besides, there were a great many of the common people of London that sympathized with the rioters, and wished to join them.

"They are our friends," said they. "They are striving to obtain redress for grievances which we suffer as well as they. Their cause is our cause. So let us open the gates and let them come in."

The Savoy

In the meantime, the whole population of the city were becoming more and more alarmed every hour, for the rioters were burning and destroying the suburbs, and they declared that if the Londoners did not open the gates, they would, after ravaging everything without the walls, take the city by storm, and burn and destroy everything in it. So it was finally concluded to open the gates and let the insurgents in.

They came in in an immense throng, which continued for many hours to pour over the bridge into the city, like a river of men above, flowing athwart the river of water below. As they entered the city, they divided and spread into all the diverging streets. A portion of them stormed a jail, and set all the prisoners free. Others marched through the streets, filling the air with dreadful shouts and outcries, and brandishing their pikes with great fury. The citizens, in hopes to conciliate them, brought out food for them, and some gave them wine. On receiving these provisions, the insurgents built fires in the streets, and encamped around them, to partake of the food and refreshments which the citizens had bestowed. They were rendered more good-natured, perhaps, by this kind treatment received from the citizens, but they soon became excited by the wine which they drank, and grew more wild and noisy than ever. At length a large party of them began to move toward the palace of the Duke of Lancaster. This palace was called the Savoy. It stood on the bank of the river, between London and Westminster, and was a grand and imposing mansion.

The Duke of Lancaster was an especial object of their hatred. He was absent at this time, as has been said, being engaged in military operations on the frontiers of Scotland. The mob, however, were determined to destroy his palace, and every thing that belonged to it.

So they broke into the house, murdering all who made any resistance, and then proceeded to break and destroy every thing the palace contained. They built fires in the court-yard and in the street, and piled upon them every thing movable that would burn. The plate, and other such valuables as would not burn, they broke up and threw into the Thames. They strictly forbade that any of the property should be taken away. One man hid a silver cup in his bosom, intending to purloin it; but he was detected in the act, and his comrades threw him, cup and all, as some say, upon the fire; others say they threw him into the Thames; at any rate, they destroyed him and his booty together.

"We are here," said they, "in the cause of truth and righteousness, to execute judgment upon a criminal, and not to become thieves and robbers ourselves."

When they had destroyed everything that the palace contained, they set fire to the building, and burned it to the ground. A portion of the walls remained standing afterward for a long time, a desolate and melancholy ruin.

The insurgents felt a special animosity against lawyers, whom they considered mercenary instruments in the hands of the nobles for oppressing them. They hung all the lawyers that they could get into their hands, and after burning the Savoy they went to the Temple, which was a spacious edifice containing the courts, the chambers of the barristers, and a vast store of ancient legal records. They burned and destroyed the whole.

Ruins of the Savoy

It is said, too, that there was a certain man in London, a rich citizen, named Richard Lyon, who had formerly been Walter the Tiler's master, and had beaten him and otherwise treated him in a cruel and oppressive manner. At the time that he received these injuries Walter had no redress, but now the opportunity had come, he thought, for revenge. So he led a gang of the most desperate and reckless of the insurgents to Lyon's house, and, seizing their terrified victim, they dragged him out without mercy, and cut off his head. The head they stuck upon the top of a pike, and paraded it through the streets, a warning, as they said, to all cruel and oppressive masters.

A great many other heads, principally those of men who had made themselves particularly obnoxious to the insurgents, were paraded through the streets in the same manner.

After spending the day in these excesses, keeping all London in a state of dreadful confusion and alarm, the various bands began to move toward night in the direction of the Tower, where the king and his court had shut themselves up in great terror, not knowing what to do to escape from the dreadful inundation of poverty and misery which had so suddenly poured in upon them. The rioters, when they reached the Tower, took possession of a large open square before it, and, kindling up great bonfires, they began to make arrangements for bivouacking there for the night.

10

The End of the Insurrection

A.D. 1381

Anxiety and embarrassment of the king.—Consultations in the Tower.—Various counsels.—Mile-End.—A meeting appointed with the rioters at Mile-End.—The king meets the insurgents at Mile-End.—Parley with them.—The king accedes to their demands.—Effect of the concessions.—Preparation of the decrees.—Scenes in the night in and around London.—The next morning.—The king meets the insurgents at Smithfield.—Another parley.—Walter advances.—His orders to his men.—Doubt about the fairness of the accounts.—Conversation between Walter and the king.—Walter gets into a quarrel with the king's squire.—Walter is at last assaulted and killed.—Excitement among his men.—Courage and coolness of the king.—Alarm conveyed to London.—Troops brought to the ground.—The insurgents surrender their banners and disperse.—The king's interview with his mother.—Final results of the rebellion.

IN the meantime, within the Tower, where the king and his courtiers now found themselves almost in a state of siege, there were continual consultations held, and much perplexity and alarm prevailed. Some of Richard's advisers recommended that the most decisive measures should be adopted at once. The king had in the Tower with him a considerable body of armed men. There were also in other parts of London and vicinity many more, amounting in all to about four thousand. It was recommended by some of the king's counselors that these men should all be ordered to attack the insurgents the next morning, and kill them without mercy. It is true that there were between fifty and one hundred thousand of the insurgents; but they had no arms, and no organization, and it was not to be expected, therefore, that they could stand a moment, numerous as they were, against the king's regular troops. They would be slaughtered, it was said, like sheep, and the insurrection would be at once put down.

Others thought that this would be a very hazardous mode of proceeding, and very uncertain as to its results.

"It is much better," said they, "that your majesty should appease them, if possible, by fair words, and by a show of granting what they ask; for if we once attempt to put them down by force, and should not be able to go through with it, we shall only make matters a great deal worse. The commonalty of London and of all England would then join them, and the nobles and the government will be swept away entirely from the land."

These counsels prevailed. It was decided not to attack the rioters immediately, but to wait a little, and see what turn things would take.

The next morning, as soon as the insurgents were in motion in the great square, they began to be very turbulent and noisy, and to threaten that they would attack the Tower itself if the king did not open the gates to them. It was finally determined to yield in part to their requests.

There was a certain place in the suburbs of London known by the name of Mile-End—so called, perhaps, because it was at the end of a mile from some place or other. At this place was an extended meadow, to which the people of London were accustomed to resort on gala days for parades and public amusements. The king sent out a messenger from the Tower to the leaders of the insurgents with directions to say to them that if they would all go to Mile-End, he would come out and meet them there.

They took him at his word, and the whole immense mass began to set itself in motion toward Mile-End.

They did not all go there, however. Those who really desired to have an interview with the king, with a view to a redress of their grievances, repaired to the appointed place of rendezvous. But of the rest, a large party turned toward London, in hopes of pillage and plunder. Others remained near the Tower. This last party, as soon as the king and his attendants had gone to Mile-End, succeeded in forcing their way in through the gates, which, it seems, had not been left properly guarded, and thus gained possession of the Tower. They ransacked the various apartments, and destroyed everything which came in their way that was at all obnoxious to them. They broke into the chamber of the Princess of Wales, Richard's mother, and, though they did not do the princess any personal injury, they terrified her so much by their violence and noise that she fainted, and was borne away apparently lifeless. Her attendants carried her down the landing-stairs on the river side, and there put her into a covered boat, and rowed her away to a place of safety.

The people in the Tower did not all get off so easily. The Archbishop of Canterbury was there, and three other prelates of high rank. These men were particularly obnoxious to the rioters, so they seized them, and without any mercy dragged them into the court and cut off their heads. The heads they put upon the ends of poles, and paraded them in this way through the streets of London.

In the meantime, the king, followed by a numerous train of attendants, had proceeded to Mile-End, and there met the insurgents, who had assembled in a vast concourse to receive him. Several of the attendants of the king were afraid to follow him into the danger to which they thought he was exposing himself by going among such an immense number of lawless and desperate men. Some of them deserted him on the way to the place of meeting, and rode off in different directions to places of safety. The king himself, however, though so young—for he was now only about sixteen years of age—had no fear. As soon as he came to the meadow at Mile-End, where the insurgents had now assembled to the number of sixteen thousand, he rode forward boldly into the midst of them, and opened the conference at once by asking them what they desired.

The spokesman whom they had appointed for the occasion stated their demands, which were that they should be made free. They had hitherto been held as serfs, in a bondage which exposed them to all sorts of cruelties and oppressions, since they were amenable, not to law, but wholly to the caprice and arbitrary will of individual masters. They demanded, therefore, that Richard should emancipate them from this bondage, and make them free.

It was determined by Richard and his counselors that this demand should be complied with, or, at least, that they should pretend to comply with it, and that decrees of emancipation for the different counties and districts which the various parties of insurgents had come from should be immediately issued. This decision seemed to satisfy them. The leaders, or at least a large portion of them, said that it was all they wanted, and several parties immediately began to set out on their return to their several homes.

But there were a great many who were not satisfied. An insurrection like this, whatever may be the object and design of the original movers in it, always brings out into prominence, and invests with temporary power, vast numbers of desperate and violent men, whose passions become inflamed by the excitement of movement and action, and by sympathy with each other, and who are never satisfied to stop with the attainment of the objects originally desired. Thus, in the present instance, although a great number of the rebels were satisfied with the promises made by the king at Mile-End, and so went home, multitudes still remained. Large parties went to London to join those who had already gone there in hopes of opportunities for pillage. Others remained at their encampments, doubting whether the king would really keep the promises which he had made them, and send the decrees. Then, besides, fresh parties of insurgents were continually arriving at London and its neighborhood, so that the danger seemed by no means to have passed away.

The king immediately caused the decree to be prepared. Thirty secretaries were employed at once to write the several copies required. They were all of the same form. They were written, as was customary with royal decrees in those times, in the Latin language, were engrossed carefully upon parchment, signed by the king, and sealed by his seal. The announcement that the secretaries were preparing these decrees, when the work had been commenced, tended greatly to satisfy the insurgents, and many more of them went home. Still, vast numbers remained, and the excitement among them, and their disposition for mischief, was evidently on the increase.

Such was the state of things during the night of Friday. The various parties of the insurgents were encamped in and around London, the glare of their fires flashing on the buildings and lighting up the sky, and their shouts, sometimes of merriment and sometimes of anger, filling the air. The peaceable inhabitants passed the night in great alarm. Some of them endeavored to conciliate the good-will of the insurgents by offering them food and wine. The wine, of course, excited them, and made them more noisy than ever. Their numbers, too, were all the time increasing, and no one could foresee how or when the trouble would end.

The next morning, a grand consultation among the rebels was determined upon. It was to be held in a great open space called Smithfield—a space set apart as a cattle-market, at the outskirts of London, toward the north. All the leaders who had not returned to their homes were present at the consultation. Among them, and at the head of them, indeed, was Wat Tyler.

The king that morning, it happened, having spent the night at the private house down the river where his mother had sought refuge after making her escape from the Tower, concluded to go to Westminster to attend mass. His real motive for making this excursion was probably to show the insurgents that he did not fear them, and also, perhaps, to make observations in respect to their condition and movements, without appearing to watch them.

He accordingly went to Westminster, accompanied and escorted by a suitable cortège and guard. The mayor of the city of London was with the party. After hearing mass at Westminster, the king set out on his return home; but, instead of going back through the heart of London, as he had come, he took a circuit to the northward by a road which, as it happened, led through Smithfield, where a great body of the insurgents had assembled, as has already been said. Thus the king came upon them quite unexpectedly both to himself and to them. When he saw them, he halted, and the horsemen who were with him halted too. There were about sixty horsemen in his train.

Some of his officers thought it would be better to avoid a re-encounter with so large a body of the insurgents—for there were about twenty thousand on the field—and recommended that the king's party should turn aside, and go home another way; but the king said "No; he preferred to speak to them."

He would go, he said, and ascertain what it was that they wanted more. He thought that by a friendly colloquy with them he could appease them.

While the king and his party thus halted to consider what to do, the attention of the leaders of the insurgents had been directed toward them. They knew at once that it was the king.

"It is the king," said Walter. "I am going to meet him and speak with him. All the rest of you are to remain here. You must not move from this spot until I come back, unless you see me make this signal."

So saying, Walter made a certain gesture with his hand, which was to be the signal for his men.

"When you see me make this signal," said he, "do you all rush forward and kill every man in the troop except the king. You must not hurt the king. We will take him and keep him. He is young, and we can make him do whatever we say. We will put him at the head of our company, as if he were our commander, and we were obeying his orders, and

THE HISTORY OF RICHARD THE SECOND

we will do everything in his name. In this way we can go wherever we please, all over England, and do what we think best, and there will be no opposition to us."

When I say that Walter gave these orders to his men, I mean that these words were attributed to him by one of the historians of the time. As, however, all the accounts which we have of these transactions were written by persons who hated the insurgents, and wished to present their case in the most unfavorable light possible, we cannot depend absolutely on the truth of their accounts, especially in cases like this, when they could not have been present to hear or see.

At any rate, Walter rode up alone to meet the king. He advanced so near to him that his horse's head touched the king's horse. While in this position, a conversation ensued between him and the king. Walter pointed to the vast concourse of men who were assembled in the field, and told the king that they were all under his orders, and that what he commanded them to do they would do. The king told him that if that were the case, he would do well to recommend them all to go to their respective homes. He had granted the petition, he said, which they had offered the day before, and had ordered decrees to be prepared emancipating them from their bondage. He asked Walter what more they required.

Walter replied that they wanted the decrees to be delivered to *them*.

"We are not willing to depart till we get all the decrees," said he. "There are all these men, and as many more besides in the city, and we wish you to give us all the decrees, that we may take them home ourselves to our several villages and towns."

The king said that the secretaries were preparing the decrees as fast as they could, and the men might depend that those which had not yet been delivered would be sent as soon as they were ready to the villages and towns.

"Go back to your men," he added, "and tell them that they had better return peaceably to their homes. The decrees will all arrive there in due time."

But Walter did not seem at all inclined to go. He looked around upon the king's attendants, and seeing one that he had known before, a squire, who was in immediate attendance on the king's person, he said to him,

"What! You here?"

This squire was the king's sword-bearer. In addition to the king's sword, which it was his duty to carry, he was armed with a dagger of his own.

Walter turned his horse toward the squire and said,

"Let me see that dagger that you have got."

"No," said the squire, drawing back.

"Yes," said the king, "let him take the dagger."

The king was not at all afraid of the rebel, and wished to let him see that he was not afraid of him.

So the squire gave Walter the dagger. Walter took it and examined it in all its parts very carefully, turning it over and over in his hands as he sat upon his horse. It was very richly ornamented, and Walter had probably never had the opportunity to examine closely anything so beautifully finished before.

After having satisfied himself with examining the dagger, he turned again to the squire:

"And now," said he, "let me see your sword."

"No," said the squire, "this is the king's sword, and it is not going into the hands of such a lowborn fellow as you. And, moreover," he added, after pausing a moment and looking at Walter with an expression of defiance, "if you and I had met somewhere alone, you would not have dared to talk as you have done, not for a heap of gold as high as this church."

There was a famous church, called the Church of St. Bartholomew, near the place where the king and his party had halted.

"By the powers," said Walter, "I will not eat this day before I have your head."

Seeing that a quarrel was impending, the mayor of London and a dozen horsemen rode up and surrounded Walter and the squire.

"Scoundrel!" said the mayor, "how dare you utter such threats as those?"

"What business is that of yours?" said Walter, turning fiercely toward the mayor. "What have you to do with it?"

"Seize him!" said the king; for the king himself was now beginning to lose his patience.

The mayor, encouraged by these words, and being already in a state of boiling indignation and rage, immediately struck a tremendous blow upon Walter's head with a cimeter which he had in his hand. The blow stunned him, and he fell heavily from his horse to the ground. One of the horsemen who had come up with the mayor—a man named John Standwich—immediately dismounted, and thrust the body of Walter through with his sword, killing him on the spot.

In the meantime, the crowd of the insurgents had remained where Walter had left them, watching the proceedings. They had received orders not to move from their position until Walter should make the signal; but when they saw Walter struck down from his horse, and stabbed as he lay on the ground, they cried out, "They have killed our captain. Form the lines! form the lines! We will go and kill every one of them."

So they hastily formed in array, and got their weapons ready, prepared to charge upon the king's party; but Richard, who in all these transactions evinced a degree of bravery and coolness very remarkable for a young man of sixteen, rode forward alone, and boldly, to meet them.

"Gentlemen," said he, "you have no leader but me. I am your king. Remain quiet and peaceable."

The insurgents seemed not to know what to do on hearing these words. Some began to move away, but the more violent and determined kept their ground, and seemed still bent on mischief. The king went back to his party, and asked them what they should do next. Some advised that they should make for the open fields, and try to escape; but the mayor of London advised that they should remain quietly where they were.

"It will be of no use," said he, "for us to try to make our escape, but if we remain here we shall soon have help."

The mayor had already sent horsemen into London to summon help. These messengers spread the cry in the city, "TO SMITHFIELD! TO SMITHFIELD! THEY ARE KILLING THE KING!" This cry produced universal excitement and alarm. The bands of armed men quartered in London were immediately turned out, and great numbers of volunteers too, seizing such weapons as they could find, made haste to march to Smithfield; and thus, in a short time, the king found himself supported by a body of seven or eight thousand men.

Some of his advisers then urged that the whole of this force should fall at once upon the insurgents, and slaughter them without mercy. This it was thought that they could easily do, although the insurgents were far more numerous than they; for the king's party consisted, in great measure, of well-armed and well-disciplined soldiers, while the insurgents were comparatively a helpless and defenseless rabble.

The king, however, would not consent to this. Perhaps somebody advised him what to do, or perhaps it was his own prudence and moderation which suggested his course. He sent messengers forward to remonstrate calmly with the men, and demand of them that they should give up their banners. If they would do so, the messengers said that the king would pardon them. So they gave up their banners. This seemed to be the signal of disbanding, and large parties of the men began to separate from the mass, and move away toward their homes.

Next, the king sent to demand that those who had received decrees of emancipation should return them. They did so; and in this way a considerable number of the decrees were given up. The king tore them to pieces on the field, upon the plea that they were forfeited by the men's having continued in rebellion after the decrees were granted.

The whole mass of the insurgents began now rapidly to get into disorder. They had no head, no banners, and the army which was gathering against them was increasing in strength and resolution every moment. The dispersal went on faster and faster, until at last those that remained threw down their weapons and fled to London.

The king then went home to his mother. She was overjoyed to see him safely returning.

"My dear son," said she, "you cannot conceive what pain and anguish I have suffered for you this day."

"Yes, mother," said Richard, "I have no doubt you have suffered a great deal. But it is all over now. Now you can rejoice and thank God, for I have regained my inheritance, the kingdom of England, which I had lost."

* * *

After this there was no farther serious trouble. The insurgents were disheartened, and most of them were glad to make the best of their way home. After the danger was past, Richard revoked all the decrees of emancipation which he had issued, on the ground that they had been extorted from him by violence and intimidation, and also that the condition on which they had been granted, namely, that the men should retire at once quietly to their homes, had not been complied with on their part. He found it somewhat difficult to recover them all, but he finally succeeded. He also sent commissions to all the towns and villages which had been implicated in the rebellion, and caused great numbers of persons to be tried and condemned to death. Many thousands were thus executed. Indeed, the rebellion had extended far and wide; for, besides the disturbances in and near London, there had been risings in all parts of the kingdom, and great excesses committed everywhere.

When the rebellion was thus quelled, things returned for a time into substantially the same condition as before, and yet the bondage of the people was never afterward so abject and hopeless as it had been. A considerable general improvement was the result. Indeed, such outbreaks as this against oppression are like the earthquakes of South America, which, though they cause for the time great terror, and often much destruction, still have the effect to raise the general level of the land, and leave it forever afterward in a better condition than before.

The cause of these rebels, moreover, badly as they managed it, was in the main a just cause; and it is to precisely such convulsive struggles as these, that have been made from time to time by the common people of England in the course of their history, that their descendants, the present commons of England and the people of America, are indebted for the personal rights and liberties which they now enjoy.

11

Good Queen Anne

A.D. 1382-1394

The planning of Richard's first marriage.—Journey of the bridal party toward England.—Their way is cut off by sea.—The bride enters Calais. —Great display.—The bride arrives in England.—Great excitement in London.—A contrast.—The bride enters London.—Parades and rejoicings.—Character of the queen.—Why she was called Good Queen Anne.—Ancient drawings.—Curious fashions of those times.—Costumes of Richard's time.—The Cracows.—Origin of the name.—The horned caps.—Description of the horns.—Pins.—Side- saddles.—Queen Anne's useful and busy life.—Shene.—Grand celebration.—The tournament.— Knights.—Magnificence of the king's mode of life.—Death of Queen Anne.—The king inconsolable.—The funeral.—Inscription on Queen Anne's tomb.

KING RICHARD was married twice. His first queen was named Anne. She was a Bohemian princess, and so is sometimes called in history Anne of Bohemia. She was, however, more commonly called Good Queen Anne.

The marriage was planned by Richard's courtiers and counselors when Richard himself was about fifteen years old. The negotiations were interrupted by the troubles connected with the insurrection described in the two last chapters; but immediately after the insurrection was quelled they were renewed. The proposals were sent to Bohemia by Richard's government. After suitable inquiries had been made by Anne's parents and friends, the proposals were accepted, and preparations were made for sending Anne to England to be married. Richard was now about sixteen years of age. Anne was fifteen. Neither of them had ever seen the other.

In due time, when everything had been made ready, the princess set out on her journey, accompanied by a large train of attendants. She was under the charge of a nobleman named the Duke of Saxony, and of his wife the duchess. The duchess was Anne's aunt. Besides the duke, there were in the party a number of knights, and other persons of distinction, and also several young ladies of the court, who went to accompany and wait upon the princess. There were also many other attendants of lower degree.

The party traveled slowly, as was the custom in those days, until at length they reached Flanders. Here, at Brussels, the capital, the princess was received by the Duke and Duchess of Brabant, who were her relatives, and was entertained by them in a very sumptuous manner. She, however, heard alarming news at Brussels. The intention of the party had been to take ship on the coast of Flanders, and proceed to Calais by water. Calais was then in the hands of the English, and an embassador with a grand suite had been sent from Richard's court to receive the princess on her arrival there, and conduct her across the Channel to Dover, and thence to London.

The reason why the princess and her party did not propose to go by land all the way to Calais was that, by so doing, they would necessarily pass through the territories of the King of France, and they were afraid that the French government would intercept them. It was known that the government of France had been opposed to the match, as tending to give Richard too much influence on the Continent.

But now, on their arrival at Brussels, the bridal party learned that there was a fleet of Norman vessels, ten or twelve in number, that were cruising to and fro on the coast, between Brussels and Calais, with a view of blocking up the princess's way by sea as well as by land. Both she herself and the Duke of Saxony were much chagrined at receiving this information, and for a time they did not know what to do. At length they sent an embassage to Paris, and after some difficulties and delay they succeeded in obtaining the consent of the French government that the princess should pass through the French territories by land. The embassadors brought back a passport for her and for her party.

Although the King of France thus granted the desired permission, he did it in a very ungracious manner, for he took care to say that he yielded to the Duke of Saxony's request solely out of kindness to his good cousin Anne, and a desire to do her a favor, and not at all out of regard to the King of England.

The princess was detained a month in Brussels while they were arranging this affair, and when at last it was settled she resumed her journey, taking the road from Brussels to Calais. The Duke of Brabant accompanied her, with an escort of one hundred spearmen. This, however, was an escort of honor rather than of protection, as the duke relied mainly upon the French passport for the safety of the party.

As the party were approaching Calais, they were received at the town of Gravelines by the English embassador and his suite, who had come out from Calais to meet them. This embassador was the Earl of Salisbury. He was attended by a force of one thousand men, namely, five hundred spearmen and five hundred archers. Conducted by this grand escort, and accompanied by a large cavalcade of knights and nobles, all clad in full armor, and splendidly mounted, the princess and the ladies in her train made a magnificent entry into Calais, through the midst of a vast concourse of spectators, with trumpets sounding and banners waving, and their hearts beating high with ecstasy and delight. In passing over the drawbridge and through the gates of Calais, Anne felt an emotion of exultation and pride in thinking that she was here entering the dominions of her future husband.

The princess did not remain long in Calais. She set out on the following day for Dover. The distance across is about twenty miles. They were dependent wholly on the wind in those days for crossing the Channel; but the princess had a prosperous passage, and arrived safely at Dover that night. News then spread rapidly all over the country, and ran up to London, that the queen had come.

The news, of course, produced universal excitement. No certain tidings of the movements of the bride had been heard for some weeks before, and no one could tell when to expect her. Her arrival awakened universal joy. Parliament was in session at the time. They voted a large sum of money to be expended in arrangements for receiving the young queen in a proper manner, and in public rejoicings on the occasion. They then immediately adjourned, and all the world began to prepare for the arrival of the royal cortège in London.

The princess, after resting a day in Dover, moved on to Canterbury, admiring, as she journeyed, the beautiful scenery of the country over which she was henceforth to be queen. Richard's uncle Thomas, the Duke of Gloucester, with a large retinue, was ready there to receive her. He conducted her to London. As they approached the city, the lord-mayor of London and all the great civic functionaries, with a long train of attendants, came out in great state to receive her and escort her into town. The place of their meeting with her was Blackheath, the same place which a year before had been the bivouac of the immense horde of ragged and miserable men that Wat Tyler and his fellow-insurgents had brought to London. But how changed now was the scene! Then the country was excited by the deepest anxiety and alarm, and the spectacle on the field was that of one immense mass of squalid poverty and wretchedness, of misery reduced by hopeless suffering to recklessness and despair. Now all was gayety and splendor in the spectacle, and the whole country was excited to the highest pitch of exultation and joy.

At Blackheath the grand cavalcade was formed for passing through London. Splendid preparations had been made in London to receive the bride, and to do honor to her passage through the city. Many of these preparations were similar to those which had been made on the occasion of the king's coronation. There was a castle and tower, with young girls at the top throwing down a shower of golden snow, and fountains at the sides flowing with wine, with fancifully-dressed pages attending to offer the princess drink from golden cups. In a word, the young and beautiful bride was received by the civic authorities of London with the same tokens of honor and the same public rejoicings that had been accorded to the king.

In a few days the marriage took place. The ceremony was performed in the chapel royal of the king's palace at Westminster. The king appeared to be very much pleased with his bride, and paid her great attention. After a week spent with her and the court in festivities and rejoicings in Westminster, he took her up the river to the royal castle at Windsor. His mother, the Princess of Wales, and other ladies of rank, went with them, and formed part of their household. They lived here very happily together for some time.

The young queen soon began to evince those kind and gracious qualities of heart which afterward made her so beloved among the people of England. Instead of occupying herself solely with her own greatness and grandeur, and with the uninterrupted round of pleasures to which her husband invited her, she began very soon to think of the sufferings which she found that a great many of the common people of England were enduring, and to consider what she could do to relieve them. The condition of the people was particularly unhappy at this time, for the king and the nobles were greatly exasperated against them on account of the rebellion, and were hunting out all who could be proved, or were even suspected to have been engaged in it, and persecuting them in the most severe and oppressive manner, and they were bloody and barbarous beyond precedent. The young queen, hearing of these things, was greatly distressed, and she begged the king, for her sake, to grant a general pardon to all his subjects, on the occasion of her coronation, which ceremony was now soon to be performed. The king granted this request, and thus peace and tranquility were once more fully restored to the land.

After this, during all her life, Anne watched for every opportunity to do good, and she was continually engaged in gentle but effective efforts to heal dissensions, to assuage angry feelings, and to alleviate suffering. She was a general peacemaker; and her lofty position, and the great influence which she exercised over the king, gave her great power to accomplish the benevolent purposes which the kindness of her heart led her to form.

The arrival of the young queen produced a great sensation among the ladies of Richard's court, in consequence of the new fashions which she introduced into England. The fashions of dress in those days were very peculiar. We learn what they were from the pictures, drawn with the pen or painted in watercolors, in the manuscripts of those days that still remain in the old English libraries. There are a great many of these drawings, and, as they agree together in the style and fashion of the costumes represented, there is no doubt that they give us correct ideas of the dresses really worn. Besides, there are many allusions in the chronicles of those times, and in poems and books of accounts, which correspond precisely with the drawings, and thus confirm their correctness and accuracy.

The engravings on the following page are copied from one of these ancient manuscripts.

Observe the singular forms of the caps, both those of the men and of the women. The men wore sometimes jackets, and sometimes long gowns which came down to the ground. The most singular feature of the dresses of the men, however, is the long-pointed shoes. Were it not that fashions are often equally absurd at the present day, we should think it impossible that such shoes as these could ever have been made.

Male Costume in the Time of Richard II

These shoes were called Cracows. Cracow was a town in Poland which was at that time within the dominions of Anne's father, and it is supposed that the fashion of wearing these shoes may have been brought into England by some of the gentlemen in Anne's train, when she came to England to be married. It is known that the queen did introduce a great many foreign fashions to the court, and, among the rest, a fashion of head-dress for ladies, which was quite as strange as peaked shoes for the gentlemen. It consisted of what was called the horned cap.

These horns were often two feet high, and sometimes two feet wide from one side to the other. The frame of this head-dress was made of wire and pasteboard, and the covering was of some glittering tissue or gauze. There were other head-dresses scarcely less monstrous than these. Some of them are represented in the engraving. These fashions, when introduced by the queen, spread with great rapidity among all the court ladies, and thence to all fashionable circles in England.

It is said, too, that it was this young queen who first introduced pins into England. Dresses had been fastened before by little skewers made of wood or ivory. Queen Anne brought pins, which had been made for some time in Germany, and the use of them soon extended all over England.

THE HISTORY OF RICHARD THE SECOND

Fashionable Head-Dresses

Side-saddles for ladies on horseback were a third fashion which Queen Anne is said to have introduced. The side-saddle which she brought was, however, of a very simple construction. It consisted of a seat placed upon the horse's back, with a sort of step depending from it on one side for the feet to rest upon. Both feet were placed upon this step together.

Queen Anne, after her marriage, lived very happily with her husband for twelve years. She was devotedly attached to him, and he seems sincerely to have loved her. He was naturally kind and affectionate in his disposition, and, while Anne lived, he yielded himself to the good influences which she exerted over him. She journeyed with him wherever he went, and aided him in the accomplishment of all his plans. Whenever he became involved in any difficulty, either with his nobles or with his subjects, she acted the part of mediator, and almost always succeeded in allaying the animosity and healing the feud before it proceeded to extremes. She resided with her husband sometimes at one palace and sometimes at another, but her favorite residence was at the palace of Shene, near the present town of Richmond.

Although the king was crowned at the time of his accession to the throne, he did not fully assume the government at that time on account of his youth, for you will remember that he was then only about eleven years old; nor did he, in fact, come fully into possession of power at the time of his marriage, for he was then under sixteen. At that time, and for several years afterward, his uncles and the other influential nobles managed the government in his name. At length, however, when he was about twenty-one years old, he thought it was time for him to assume the direction of affairs himself, and he accordingly did so. At this time there was another grand celebration, one scarcely inferior in pomp and splendor to the coronation itself.

Among other performances on this occasion there was a tournament, in which knights mounted on horseback, and armed from head to foot with iron armor, fought in the lists, endeavoring to unhorse each other by means of their spears. The tournament was held at Smithfield. Raised platforms were set up by the side of the lists for the lords and ladies of the court, and a beautiful canopy for the queen, who was to act as judge of the combat, and was to award the prizes. The prizes consisted of a rich jeweled clasp and a splendid crown of gold.

The queen went first to the ground, and took her place with her attendants under her canopy. The knights who were to enter the lists then came in a grand cavalcade through the streets of London to the palace. There were sixty ladies mounted on beautiful palfreys, accoutred with the new-fashioned side-saddles. Each of these ladies conducted a knight, whom she led by a silver chain. They were preceded by minstrels and bands of instrumental music, and the streets were thronged with spectators.

After the tournament there was a grand banquet at the palace of the Bishop of London, with music and dancing, and other such amusements, which continued to a late hour of the night.

* * *

For some years after this the king and queen lived together in great prosperity. Outwardly things went pretty well with the king's affairs, and, as he was fond of pomp and display, he gradually acquired habits of very profuse and lavish expenditure. Indeed, he is said to have made it an object of his ambition to surpass, in the magnificence of his style of living, all the sovereigns of Europe. He kept many separate establishments in his different palaces, and at all of them gave entertainments and banquets of immense magnificence and of the most luxurious character. It is said that three hundred persons were employed in his kitchens.

At length, in the year 1394, when Richard was preparing for an expedition into Ireland to quell a rebellion which had broken out there, the queen was seized with a fatal epidemic which was then prevailing in England, and after a short illness she died. She was at her palace of Shene at this time. The king hastened to attend her the moment that he heard the tidings of her illness, and was with her when she died. He was inconsolable at the loss of his wife, for he had loved her sincerely, and she had been a singularly faithful and devoted wife to him. He was made almost crazy by her death. He imprecated bitter curses on the palace where she died, and he ordered it to be destroyed. It was, in fact, partially dismantled, in obedience to these orders, and Richard himself never occupied it again. It was, however, repaired under a subsequent reign.

Richard gave up, for the time being, his expedition into Ireland, being wholly absorbed in his sorrow for the irreparable loss he had suffered. He wrote letters to all the great nobles and barons of England to come to the funeral, and the obsequies were celebrated with the greatest possible pomp and parade. Two months were expended in making preparations for the funeral. When the day arrived, a very long procession was formed to escort the body from Shene to Westminster. This procession was accompanied by an immense number of torch-bearers, all carrying lighted torches in their hands. So great was the number of these torches, that a large quantity of wax was imported from Flanders expressly for the purpose.

The tomb of Anne was not made until a year after her death. Richard himself attended to all the details connected with the construction of it. The inscription was in Latin. The following is an exact translation of it:

> "Under this stone lies Anne, here entombed,
> Wedded in this world's life to the second Richard.
> To Christ were her meek virtues devoted:
> His poor she freely fed from her treasures;
> Strife she assuaged, and swelling feuds appeased;
> Beauteous her form, her face surpassing fair.
> On July's seventh day, thirteen hundred ninety-four,
> All comfort was bereft, for through irremediable sickness
> She passed away into interminable joys."

By the death of his wife, Richard was left, as it were, almost alone in the world. His mother, the Princess of Wales, had died some time before, and Anne had had no children. There were his uncles and his cousins, it is true, but they were his rivals and competitors rather than his friends. Indeed, they were destined soon to become his open enemies.

Richard was afterward married again, to his "little wife," as we shall see in a future chapter.

12

Incidents of the Reign

A.D. 1382-1396

Jealousy of Richard and his mother against the uncles.—Plots and manoeuvres.—Thomas, Duke of Gloucester.—Province of Parliament.—Prerogative of the king.—The Commons threaten the king.—He is compelled to yield.—Council appointed.—Richard's discontent.—The court at Nottingham.—Preparations for war.—Richard and his party overcome.—Execution of Burley.—Queen Anne's fruitless intercession.—The king determines to resume his power.—His interview with his council.—Surprise of the barons.—The great seal.—Richard appoints a new chancellor.—Richard appoints new officers of government.—The wars in which Richard was engaged.—Story of Sir Miles, the Bohemian knight.—The archers and the squires.—A squire killed.—Sir Ralph Stafford is displeased and alarmed.—Lord Holland is enraged.—He meets Lord Stafford in a narrow lane.—Stafford is killed.—Lord Holland's unconcern.—Richard's perplexity and distress.—His mother's anguish.—Extraordinary marriage of the Duke of Lancaster.—Indignation and rage of the ladies of the court.

IN giving some general account of the character of Richard's reign, and of the incidents that occurred during the course of it, we now go back a little again, so as to begin at the beginning of it.

When Richard was married, he was, as has already been said, only about fifteen or sixteen years of age. As he grew older, after this time, and began to feel that sense of strength and independence which pertains to manhood, he became more and more jealous of the power and influence of his uncles in the government of the country. His mother, too, who was still living, and who adhered closely to him, was very suspicious of the uncles. She was continually imagining that they were forming plots and conspiracies against her son in favor of themselves or of their own children. She was particularly suspicious of the Duke of Lancaster, and of his son Henry Bolingbroke. It proved in the end that there was some reason for this suspicion, for this Henry Bolingbroke was the means at last of deposing Richard from his throne in order to take possession of it himself, as we shall see in the sequel.

In order to prevent, as far as possible, these uncles from finding opportunity to accomplish any of their supposed designs, Richard and his mother excluded them, as much as they could, from power, and appointed other persons, who had no such claims to the crown, to all the important places about the court. This, of course, made the uncles very angry. They called the men whom Richard thus brought forward his favorites, and they hated them exceedingly. This state of things led to a great many intrigues, and manoeuvres, and plots, and counterplots, the favorites against the uncles, and the uncles against the favorites. These difficulties were continued for many years. Parties were formed in Parliament, of which sometimes one was in the ascendency and sometimes the other, and all was turmoil and confusion.

When Richard was about twenty years old, one of his uncles—his uncle Thomas, at that time Duke of Gloucester—gained such an influence in Parliament that some of Richard's favorites were deposed from office and imprisoned. The duke was imboldened by this success to take a farther step. He told the Parliament that the government would never be on a good footing until they themselves appointed a council to manage in the king's name.

THE HISTORY OF RICHARD THE SECOND

When Richard heard of this plan, he declared that he would never submit to it.

"I am the King of England," said he, "and I will govern my realm by means of such officers as I choose to appoint myself. I will not have others to appoint them for me."

The ideas which the kings of those days entertained in respect to the province of Parliament was that it was to vote the necessary taxes to supply the king's necessities, and also to mature the details of all laws for the regulation of the ordinary business and the social relations of life, but that the government, strictly so called—that is, all that relates to the appointment and payment of executive officers, the making of peace or war, the building and equipment of fleets, and the command of armies, was exclusively the king's prerogative, and that for the exercise of his prerogative in these particulars the sovereign was responsible, not to his subjects, but to God alone, from whom he claimed to have received his crown.

The people of England, as represented by Parliament, have never consented to this view of the subject. They have always maintained that their kings are, in some sense, responsible to the people of the realm, and they have often deposed kings, and punished them in other ways.

Accordingly, when Richard declared that he would not submit to the appointment of a council by Parliament, the Commons reminded him of the fact that his great-grandfather, Edward the Second, had been deposed in consequence of having unreasonably and obstinately resisted the will of his people, and they hinted to him that it would be well for him to beware lest he should incur the same fate. Some of the lords, too, told him that the excitement was so great in the country on account of the mismanagement of public affairs, and the corruptions and malpractice of the favorites, that if he refused to allow the council to be appointed, there was danger that he would lose his head.

So Richard was obliged to submit, and the council was appointed. Richard was in a great rage, and he secretly determined to lay his plans for recovering the power into his own hands as soon as possible, and punishing the council, and all who were concerned in appointing them, for their audacity in presuming to encroach in such a manner upon his sovereign rights as king.

The council that was appointed consisted of eleven bishops and nobles. Richard's uncle Thomas, the Duke of Gloucester, was at the head of it. This council governed the country for more than a year. Everything was done in Richard's name, it is true, but the real power was in the hands of the Duke of Gloucester. Richard was very angry and indignant, but he did not see what he could do.

He was, however, all the time forming plans and schemes to recover his power. At last, after about a year had passed away, he called together a number of judges secretly at Nottingham, toward the northern part of the kingdom, and submitted to them the question whether such a council as the Parliament had appointed was legal. It was, of course, understood beforehand how the judges would decide. They decreed that the council was illegal; that for Parliament to give a council such powers was a violation of the king's prerogative, and was consequently treason, and that, of course, all who had been concerned in the transaction had made themselves liable to the penalty of death.

It was Richard's plan, after having obtained this decree, to cause the prominent members of the council to be arrested, and he came to London and began to make his preparations for accomplishing this purpose. But as soon as his uncle Thomas, the Duke of Gloucester, heard of these plans, he, and some great nobles who were ready to join with him against the king, collected all their forces, and began to march to London at the head of forty thousand men. Richard's cousin Henry, the Duke of Lancaster's son, joined them on the way. Richard's friends and favorites, on hearing of this, immediately took arms, and preparations began to be made for civil war. In a word, after having successfully met and quelled the great insurrection of the serfs and laborers under Wat Tyler, Richard was now to encounter a still more formidable resistance of his authority on the part of his uncles and the great barons of the realm. These last, indeed, were far more to be feared than the others, for they had arms and organization, and they enjoyed every possible facility for carrying on a vigorous and determined war. Richard and his party soon found that it was useless to attempt to resist them. Accordingly, after a very brief struggle, the royal party was entirely put down. Richard's favorites were arrested. Some of them were beheaded, others were banished from the realm, and the government of the country fell again into the hands of the uncles.

One of Richard's favorites who was executed on this occasion was a man whose untimely death grieved and afflicted both Richard and the queen very much indeed. His name was Sir Simon Burley. He had been Richard's friend and companion all his life. Richard's father, Edward, the Black Prince, had appointed Sir Simon Richard's tutor while Richard himself was a mere child, and he had been with him ever since that time. Queen Anne was much attached to him, and she was particularly grateful to him on account of his having been the commissioner who negotiated and arranged her marriage with Richard. Richard made every possible exertion to save his tutor's life, but his uncle Gloucester was inexorable. He told Richard that his keeping the crown depended on the immediate execution of the traitor. Queen Anne fell on her knees before him, and begged and entreated that Sir Simon might be spared, but all was of no avail.

So Richard was compelled to submit; but he did not do so without secret muttering, and resolutions of revenge. He allowed the government to remain in his uncle's hands for some time, but at length, about a year afterward, he found himself strong enough to seize it again. The plea which his uncles had hitherto made for managing the government themselves was, that Richard was not yet of age. But now he became of age, and he resolved on what might be called a *coup d'état*, to get possession of the government. He planned this measure in concert with a number of his own friends and favorites, who hoped, by this means, that they themselves should rise to power.

He called a grand council of all the nobles and great officers of state. The assembly convened in the great council-chamber, and waited there for the king to come in.

At length the king arrived, and, walking into the chamber, he took his seat upon the throne. A moment afterward he turned to one of the chief officers present and addressed him, saying,

"My lord, what is my age at the present time?"

The nobleman answered that his majesty was now over twenty years of age.

"Then," said the king, speaking in a very firm and determined manner, "I am of years sufficient to govern mine own house and family, and also my kingdom; for it seemeth against reason that the state of the meanest person in my kingdom should be better than mine. Every heir throughout the land that has once come to the age of twenty years is permitted, if his father be not living, to order his business himself. And that which is permitted by law to every other person, of however mean degree, why is it denied to me?"

The king spoke these words with an air of such courage and determination that the barons were astonished. The foremost of them, after a brief pause, seemed ready to accede to his proposals. They said that there should henceforth be no right abridged from him, but that he might take upon himself the government if he chose, as it was now manifestly his duty to do.

"Very well," said the king. "You know that I have been a long time ruled by tutors and governors, so that it has not been lawful for me to do anything, no matter of how small importance, without their consent. Now, therefore, I desire that henceforth they meddle no more with matters pertaining to my government, for I will attend to them myself, and after the manner of an heir arrived at full age. I will call whom I please to be my counsel, and thus manage my own affairs according to my own will and pleasure."

The barons were extremely surprised to hear these determinations thus resolutely announced by the king, but had nothing to say in reply.

"And in the first place," continued Richard, "I wish the chancellor to give me up the great seal."

The great seal was a very important badge and emblem of the royal prerogative. No decree was of legal authority until an impress from this seal was attached to it. The officer who had charge of it was called the chancellor. A new seal was prepared for each sovereign on his accession to the throne. The devices were much the same in all. They consisted of a representation of the king seated on his throne upon one side of the seal, and on the other mounted on horseback and going into battle, armed from head to foot. The legends or inscriptions around the border were changed, of course, for each reign.

The engraving on the following page represents one side of king Richard's seal. The other side contained an image of the king seated on his throne, and surrounded by various insignia of royalty.

"I wish the chancellor," said the king, "to deliver me up the great seal."

So the nobleman who had been chancellor up to that time delivered the seal into the hands of the king. The seal was kept in a beautiful box, richly ornamented. It was always brought to the council by the lord chancellor, who had it in charge. The king proceeded immediately afterward to appoint a new chancellor, and to place the box in his hands. In the same summary manner the king displaced almost

The Seal Of Richard II

all the other high officers of state, and appointed new ones of his own instead of them. The former officers were obliged to submit, though sorely against their will. They were powerless, for the king had now attained such an age that there was no longer any excuse for withholding from him the complete possession of his kingdom.

From this time, accordingly, Richard was actually as well as nominally king of England; but still he was often engaged in contentions and quarrels with his uncles, and with the other great nobles who took his uncle's part.

The queen—for good Queen Anne was at this time still living—was so gentle and kind, and she acted her part as peacemaker so well, that she greatly softened and soothed these asperities; but Richard led, nevertheless, a wild and turbulent life, and was continually getting involved in the most serious difficulties. Then there were wars to be carried on, sometimes with France, sometimes with Scotland, and sometimes with Ireland. Richard's uncles, the Dukes of Lancaster and Gloucester, generally went away in command of the armies to carry on these wars. Sometimes Richard himself accompanied the expeditions; but even on these occasions, when he and his knights and nobles were engaged together in a common cause, and apparently at peace with each other, there were so many jealousies and angry heartburnings among them, that deadly quarrels and feuds were continually breaking out.

As an example of these quarrels, I will give an account of one which took place not very long after Richard was married. He was engaged with his uncles in an expedition to Scotland. There was a knight in attendance upon him named Sir Miles. This knight was a friend of the queen. He was a Bohemian, and had come from Bohemia to pay Anne a visit, and to bring the news to her from her native land. The king, out of affection to Anne, paid him great attention. This made the English knights and nobles jealous, and they amused themselves with mimicking and laughing at Sir Miles's foreign peculiarities. The particular friends of the queen, however, took his part, one especially, named the Earl of Stafford, and his son, the young Lord Ralph Stafford. Lord Ralph Stafford was one of the most courteous and popular knights in England.

In the course of the expedition to Scotland the party came to a town called Beverley, which is situated in the northern part of England, near the frontier. One day, two archers belonging to the service of Lord

THE HISTORY OF RICHARD THE SECOND

Ralph Stafford, in riding across the fields near Beverley, found two squires engaged in a sort of quarrel with Sir Miles. The cause of the quarrel was something about his lodgings in the town. The squires, it seems, knowing that the knights and nobles generally disliked Sir Miles, were encouraged to be very bold and insolent to him in expressing their ill-will, and when the archers came up they were following him with taunts, and ridicule, and abuse, while Sir Miles was making the best of his way toward the town.

The archers took the Bohemian's part. They remonstrated with the squires for thus abusing and teasing a stranger and a foreigner, a personal friend, too, and guest of the queen.

"What business is it of yours, villainous knave, whether we laugh at him or not?" said the squires. "What right have you to intermeddle? What is it to you?"

"What is it to us?" repeated one of the archers. "It is a great deal to us. This man is the friend of our master, and we will not stand by and see him abused."

Upon hearing this, one of the squires uttered some words of defiance, and advanced as if to strike the archer; but the archer, having his bow and arrow all ready, suddenly let the arrow fly, and the squire was killed on the spot.

Sir Miles had already gone on toward the town. The other squire, seeing his companion dead, immediately made his escape. The two archers, leaving the man whom they had killed on the ground where he had fallen, made the best of their way home, and told their master, Sir Ralph Stafford, what they had done.

Sir Ralph was extremely concerned to hear of the occurrence, and he told the archer who killed the squire that he had done very wrong.

"But, my lord," said the archer, "I could not have done otherwise; for the man was coming up to us with his sword drawn in his hand, and we were obliged either to kill him or to be killed ourselves."

The archers, moreover, told Sir Ralph that the squires were in the service of Sir John Holland. Now Sir John Holland was a half brother of the king, being the child of his mother, the Princess of Wales, by a former husband. When Sir Ralph heard this, he was still more alarmed than before. He told the archers who killed the squire that they must go and hide themselves somewhere until the affair could be arranged.

"I will negotiate with Lord Holland for your pardon," said he, "either through my father or in some other way. But, in the mean time, you must keep yourselves closely concealed."

The Earl of Stafford, Lord Ralph Stafford's father, was a nobleman of the very highest rank, and of great influence.

It is a curious indication of the ideas that prevailed in those days, and of the relations that subsisted between the nobles and their dependants, that the slaughter of a man in an affray of this kind was a matter to be *arranged* between the masters respectively of the men engaged in it.

The archers went away to hide themselves until Lord Ralph could arrange the matter.

In the mean time, the squire who had escaped in the fray hurried home and related the matter to Lord Holland. Lord Holland was greatly enraged. He uttered dreadful imprecations against Lord Ralph Stafford and against Sir Miles, whom he seemed to consider responsible for the death of his squire, and declared that he would not sleep until he had had his revenge. So he mounted his horse, and, taking some trusty attendants with him, rode into Beverley, and asked where Sir Miles's lodgings were. While he was going toward the place, breathing fury and death, suddenly, in a narrow lane, he came upon Lord Ralph, who was then going to find him, in order to arrange about the murder. It was now, however, late in the evening, and so dark that the parties did not at first know each other.

"Who comes here?" said Lord Holland, when he saw Sir Ralph approaching.

"I am Stafford," replied Sir Ralph.

"You are the very man I want to see," said Lord Holland. "One of your servants has killed my squire—the one that I loved so much."

As he said this, he brought down so heavy a blow upon Sir Ralph's head as to fell him from his horse to the ground. He then rode on. The attendants hurried to the spot and raised Sir Ralph up. They found him faint and bleeding, and in a few moments he died.

As soon as this fact was ascertained, one of the men rode on after Lord Holland, and, coming up to him, said,

"My lord, you have killed Lord Stafford."

"Very well," said Lord Holland; "I am glad of it. I would rather it would be a man of his rank than any body else, for so I am the more completely revenged for the death of my squire."

As fast as the tidings of these events spread, they produced universal excitement. The Earl of Stafford, the father of Sir Ralph, was plunged into the most inconsolable grief at the death of his son. The earl was one of the most powerful nobles in the army, and, if he had undertaken to avenge himself on Lord Holland, the whole expedition would perhaps have been broken up into confusion. On the king's solemn assurance that Holland would be punished, he was appeased for the time; but then the Princess of Wales, Richard's mother, who was Lord Holland's mother too, was thrown into the greatest state of anxiety and distress. She implored Richard to save his brother's life. All the other nobles and knights took sides too in the quarrel, and for a time it seemed that the dissension would never be healed. Lord Holland, in the mean while, fled to the church at Beverley, and took sanctuary there. By the laws and customs of the time, they could not touch him until he came voluntarily out.

Richard resisted all the entreaties of his mother to spare the murderer's life until he found that her anxiety and distress were preying upon her health so much that he feared that she would die. At last, to save his mother's life, he promised that Holland should be spared. But it was too late. His mother fell into a decline, and at length died, as it was said, of a broken heart. What a dreadful death! that of a mother worn out by the agony of long-continued and apparently fruitless efforts to prevent one of her children from being the executioner of another for the crime of murder.

Besides these fierce, deadly contests among the knights and nobles, the ladies of the court had their feuds and quarrels too. They were often divided into cliques and parties, and were full of envyings, jealousies, and resentments against each other. One of the most serious of these difficulties was occasioned by a marriage of the Duke of Lancaster, which took place toward the close of his life. This was his third marriage, he having been successively married to two ladies of high rank before. The lady whom he now married was of a comparatively humble station in life. She was the daughter of a foreign knight. Her name, originally, was Catharine de Rouet. She had been, in her early life, a maiden in attendance on the Duchess of Lancaster, the duke's second wife. While she was in his family the duke formed a guilty intimacy with her, which was continued for a long time. They had three children. The duke provided well for these children, and gave them a good education. After a time, the duke, becoming tired of her, arranged for her to be married to a certain knight named Swinton, and she lived with this knight for some time, until at length he died, and Catharine became a widow.

The Duchess of Lancaster died also, and then the duke became for the second time a widower, and he now conceived the idea of making Catharine Swinton his wife. His motive for this was not his love for *her*, for that, it is said, had passed away, but his regard for the children, who, on the marriage of their mother to the father of the children, would be legitimatized, and would thus become entitled to many legal rights and privileges from which they would otherwise be debarred. The other ladies of the court, however, particularly the wives of the other dukes —the Duke of Lancaster's brothers—were greatly incensed when they heard of this proposed marriage, and they did all they possibly could do to prevent it. All was, however, of no avail, for the Duke of Lancaster was not a man to be easily thwarted in any determination that he might take into his head. So he was married, and the poor despised Catharine was made the first duchess in the realm, and became entitled to take precedence of all the other duchesses.

This the other duchesses could not endure. They could not bear it, they said, and they *would* not bear it. They declared that they would not go into any place where this woman, as they called her, was to be. As might have been expected, an interminable amount of quarreling and ill-will grew out of this affair.

About the time of this marriage of the duke, the king himself was married a second time, as will be related in the next chapter.

13

The Little Queen

A.D. 1395-1396

Some account of Isabella of France, the little queen.—Richard opens negotiations with the King of France.—A grand embassage sent to France.—Their reception.—Interview of the embassadors with little Isabella.—The negotiations go on satisfactorily.—The marriage ceremony is performed by proxy.—Richard makes arrangements to go and receive his bride.—Grand preparations for the expedition.—The meeting on the French frontier.—The pavilions.—Precautions to guard against violence or treachery.—Ceremonious interviews.—Grand entertainment.—Richard receives his bride.—The palanquin.—Excitement in London.—Reception of the little queen.—The little queen's mode of life in England.

KING RICHARD'S second wife was called the little queen, because she was so young and small when she was married. She was only about nine years old at that time. The story of this case will show a little how the marriages of kings and princesses in those days were managed.

It was not long after the death of good Queen Anne before some of Richard's courtiers and counselors began to advise him to be married again. He replied, as men always do in such cases, that he did not know where to find a wife. The choice was indeed not very large, being restricted by etiquette to the royal families of England and of the neighboring countries. Several princesses were proposed one after another, but Richard did not seem to like any of them. Among other ladies, one of his cousins was proposed to him, a daughter of the Duke of Gloucester. But Richard said no; she was too nearly related to him.

At last he took it into his head that he should like to marry little Isabella, the Princess of France, then about nine years old. The idea of his being married to Isabella was calculated to surprise people for two reasons: first, because Isabella was so small, and, secondly, because the King of France, her father, was Richard's greatest and most implacable enemy. France and England had been on bad terms with each other not only during the whole of Richard's reign, but through a great number of reigns preceding; and now, just before the period when this marriage was proposed, the two nations had been engaged in a long and sanguinary war. But Richard said that he was going to make peace, and that this marriage was to be the means of confirming it.

"But she is altogether too young for your majesty," said Richard's counselors. "She is a mere child."

"True," said the king; "but that is an objection which will grow less and less every year. Besides, I am in no haste. I am young enough myself to wait till she grows up, and, in the meantime, I can have her trained and educated to suit me exactly."

So, after a great deal of debate among the king's counselors and in Parliament, it was finally decided to send a grand embassage to Paris to propose to the King of France that he should give his little daughter Isabella in marriage to Richard, King of England.

This embassage consisted of an archbishop, two earls, and twenty knights, attended each by two squires, making forty squires in all, and five hundred horsemen. The party proceeded from London to Dover, then crossed to Calais, which was at this time an English possession, and thence proceeded to Paris.

When they arrived at Paris they entered the city with great pomp and parade, being received with great honor by the French king, and they were lodged sumptuously in quarters provided for them.

The embassadors were also very honorably received at court. The king invited them to dine with him, and entertained them handsomely, but many objections were made to the proposed marriage.

"How can we," said the French counselors, "give a Princess of France in marriage to our worst and bitterest enemy?"

To this the embassadors replied that the marriage would establish and confirm a permanent peace between the two countries.

Then there was another objection. Isabella was already engaged. She had been betrothed some time before to the son of a duke of one of the neighboring countries. But the embassadors said that they thought this could be arranged.

While these negotiations were going on, the embassadors asked permission to see the princess. This at first the king and queen, Isabella's father and mother, declined. They said that she was only eight or nine years old, and that such a child would not know at all how to conduct at such an interview.

However, the interview was granted at last. The embassadors were conducted to an apartment in the palace of the Louvre, where the princess and her parents were ready to receive them. On coming into the presence of the child, the chief embassador advanced to her, and, kneeling down before her, he said,

"Madam, if it please God, you shall be our lady and queen."

The princess looked at him attentively while he said this. She was a very beautiful child, with a gentle and thoughtful expression of countenance, and large dark eyes, full of meaning.

She replied to the embassador of her own accord in a clear, childish voice,

"Sir, if it please God and my lord and father that I be Queen of England, I should be well pleased, for I have been told that there I shall be a great lady."

Isabella then took the kneeling embassador by the hand and lifted him up. She then led him to her mother.

The embassadors were extremely pleased with the appearance and behavior of the princess, and were more than ever desirous of succeeding in their mission. But, after some farther negotiations, they received for their answer that the French court were disposed to entertain favorably the proposal which Richard made, but that nothing could be determined upon the subject at that time.

"We must wait," said the king, "until we can see what arrangement can be made in regard to the princess's present engagement, and then, if King Richard will send to us again, next spring we will give a final answer."

So slow are the movements and operations in such a case as this among the great, that the embassadors were occupied three weeks in Paris in advancing the business to this point. They were, however, well satisfied with what they had done, and at length took their leave, and returned to London in high spirits with their success, and reported the result to King Richard. He himself was well satisfied too.

The negotiations went on prosperously during the winter, and in the spring another embassage was sent, larger than the preceding. The attendants of this embassage were several thousand in number, and they occupied a whole street in Paris when they arrived there. By this embassage the arrangement of the marriage was finally concluded. The ceremony was in fact performed, for Isabella was actually married to Richard, by proxy as it is called, a customary mode of conducting marriages between a princess and a king. One of the embassadors, a grand officer of state, personated King Richard on this occasion, and the marriage was celebrated with the greatest possible pomp and splendor.

Besides the marriage contracts, there were various other treaties and covenants to be drawn up, and signed and sealed. All this business required so much time, that this embassage, like the other, remained three weeks in Paris, and then they returned home to London, and reported to Richard what they had done.

Still the affair was not yet fully settled. A great many of the nobles and the people of England very strenuously opposed the match, for they wished the war with France to be continued. This was particularly the case with Richard's uncle, the Duke of Gloucester. He had greatly distinguished himself in the war thus far, and he wished it to be continued; so he did all he could to oppose the consummation of the marriage, and the negotiations and delays were long protracted. Richard, however, persevered, and at length the obstacles were so far removed, that in the fall of 1396 he began to organize a grand expedition to go with him to the frontiers of France to receive his bride.

Immense preparations were made on both sides for the ceremonial of this visit. The meeting was to take place on the frontier, since neither sovereign dared to trust himself within the dominions of the other, for fear of treachery. For the same reason, each one deemed it necessary to take with him a very large armed force. Great stores of provisions for the expedition were accordingly prepared, and sent on beforehand; portions being sent down the Thames from London, and the rest being purchased in Flanders and other countries on the Continent, and forwarded to Calais by water. The King of France also, for the use of his party, sent stores from Paris to all the towns in the neighborhood of the frontier.

Among the ladies of the court on both sides there was universal emulation and excitement in respect to plans and preparations which they had to make for the wedding. Great numbers of them were to accompany the expedition, and nothing was talked of but the dresses and decorations which they should wear, and the parts that they should respectively perform in the grand parade. Hundreds of armorers, and smiths, and other artisans were employed in repairing and embellishing the armor of the knights and barons, and in designing and executing new banners, and new caparisons for the horses, richer and more splendid than were ever known before.

There was a great deal of heartburning and ill-will in respect to the Duke of Lancaster's new wife, with whom the other ladies of the court had declared they would not associate on any terms. The king was determined that she should go on the expedition, and the other ladies consequently found themselves obliged either to submit to her presence, or forego the grandest display which they would ever have the opportunity to witness as long as they should live. They concluded to submit, though they did it with great reluctance and with a very ill grace.

At length everything was ready, and the expedition, leaving London, journeyed to Dover, and then crossed the Straits to Calais. A long time was then consumed in negotiations in respect to the peace; for, although Richard himself was willing to make peace on almost any terms, so that he might obtain his little bride, his uncles and the other leading nobles made great difficulties, and it was a long time before the treaties could be arranged. At length, however, everything was settled, and the preparations were made for delivering to Richard his bride.

Two magnificent pavilions were erected near the frontier, one on the French and the other on the English side. These pavilions were for the use of the two monarchs respectively, and of their lords and nobles. Then, in the centre, between these, and, of course, exactly upon the frontier, a third and more open pavilion was set up. In this central pavilion the two kings were to have their first meeting. For either of the kings to have entered first into the dominions of the other would have been, in some sense, an acknowledgment of inferiority on his part. So it was contrived that neither should first visit the other, but that they should advance together, each from his own pavilion, and meet in the central one, after which they could visit each other as it might be convenient. The first interview therefore took place in the centre pavilion. It was necessary, however, to take some strong precautions against treachery. Accordingly, before the meeting, an oath was administered to both monarchs, by which each one solemnly asseverated that he was acting in good faith in this transaction, and that he had no secret reservation or treachery in his heart, and pledged his sacred honor that the other should suffer no violence, damage, molestation, arrest, constraint, or any other inconvenience whatever during the interview.

As an additional precaution, a strong force, consisting of four hundred knights on each side, all fully armed, were drawn up on opposite sides of the central pavilion, the English troops on the English side, and the French on the French side. Besides these knights, each of the kings had a strong force stationed in reserve, at a little distance from their respective pavilions, to be ready in case of any difficulty. These troops were arranged in such a manner that the King of England should pass between the ranks of the English knights in going to the pavilion, and the French king between the French knights.

Things being thus arranged, at the appointed hour the two kings set out together from their own pavilions, and walked, accompanied each by a number of dukes and nobles of high rank, to the central pavilion. Here the kings, both being uncovered, approached each other. They saluted each other in a very friendly manner, and held a brief conversation together. Some of the accounts say that the French king, then taking the English king by the hand, led him to the French tent, the French dukes who had accompanied him following with the English dukes who had accompanied Richard, and that there the whole party partook of refreshment.

However this may be, the first interview was one mainly of ceremony. Afterward there were other interviews in the different pavilions. These alternating visits were continued for several days, until at length the time was appointed for a final meeting, at which the little queen was to be delivered into her husband's hands.

This final grand ceremony took place in the French pavilion. The order of proceeding was as follows. First there was a grand entertainment. The table was splendidly laid out, and there was a sideboard loaded with costly plate. At the table the kings were waited upon by dukes. During the dinner, Richard talked with the King of France about his wife, and about the peace which was now so happily confirmed and established between the two countries.

After dinner the cloth was removed and the tables were taken away. When the pavilion was cleared a door was opened, and a party of ladies of the French court, headed by the queen, came in, conducting the little princess. As soon as she had entered, the King of France took her by the hand and led her to Richard. Richard received her with a warm welcome, and, lifting her up in his arms, kissed her. He told the King of France that he was fully sensible of the value of such a gift, and that he received it as a pledge of perpetual amity and peace between the two countries. He also, as had been previously agreed upon, solemnly renounced all claim to the throne of France on account of Isabella or her descendants, forever.

He then immediately committed the princess to the hands of the Duchess of Lancaster, and the other ladies, and they at once conveyed her to the door of the tent. Here there was a sort of palanquin, magnificently made and adorned, waiting to receive her. The princess was put into this palanquin, and immediately set out for Calais. Richard and the immense train of knights and nobles followed, and thus, at a very rapid pace, the whole party returned to Calais.

A few days after this the marriage ceremony was performed anew between Richard and Isabella, Richard himself being personally present this time. Great was the parade and great the rejoicing on this occasion. After the marriage, the little queen was again put under the charge of the Duchess of Lancaster and the other English ladies who had been appointed to receive her.

In the meantime, all London was becoming every day more and more excited in expectation of the arrival of the bridal party there. Great preparations were made for receiving them. At length, about a fortnight after taking leave of her father, Isabella arrived in London. She spent the first night at the Tower, and on the following day passed through London to Westminster in a grand procession. An immense concourse of people assembled on the occasion. Indeed, such was the eagerness of the people to see the queen on her arrival in London, that there were nine persons crushed to death by the crowd on London Bridge when she was passing over it.

The queen took up her residence at Windsor Castle, where she was under the charge of the Duchess of Lancaster and other ladies, who were to superintend her education. King Richard used to come and visit her very often, and on such occasions she was excused from her studies, and so she was always glad to see him; besides, he used to talk with her and play with her in a very friendly and affectionate manner. He was now about thirty years old, and she was ten. He, however, liked her very much, for she was very beautiful, and very amiable and affectionate in her manners. She liked to have Richard come and see her too, for his visits not only released her for the time from her studies, but he was very gentle and kind to her, and he used to play to her on musical instruments, and sing to her, and amuse her in various other ways. She admired, moreover, the splendor of his dress, for he always came in very magnificent apparel.

In a word, Richard and his little queen, notwithstanding the disparity of their years, were both very well pleased with the match which they had made. Richard was proud of the youth and beauty of his wife, and Isabella was proud of the greatness, power, and glory of her husband.

14

Richard's Deposition and Death

A.D. 1397-1399

Difficulties of Richard's position.—His rivals.—Plot discovered.—Richard arrests his uncle Gloucester.—Extraordinary circumstances of the arrest.—Richard becomes extremely unpopular.—His excesses.—Remorse. —His fear of Henry Bolingbroke.—Coventry.—Preparation for the combat.—The combat arrested.—Henry is banished from England.—Case of Lady De Courcy.—Her dismissal from office.—Richard seizes his cousin Henry's estates.—Ireland.—Richard's farewell to the little queen.—A rebellion.—Misfortunes of the king.—Conway Castle.—The king is made prisoner.—His interview with Henry at the castle in Wales.—The king is conveyed a prisoner to London.—Parliament convened.—Charges preferred against the king.—Interview between Richard and Henry in the Tower.—Rage of Richard.—Portrait of Henry.—The king is compelled to abdicate the crown.—Henry desires that Richard should be killed.— Assassination of Richard.—Disposal of the body.—The little queen.—Her return to France.—Sequel of the story of the little queen.

IT was not long after Richard's marriage to the little queen before the troubles and difficulties in which his government was involved increased in a very alarming degree. The feuds among his uncles, and between his uncles and himself, increased in frequency and bitterness, and many plots and counterplots were formed in respect to the succession; for Isabella being so young, it was very doubtful whether she would grow up and have children, and, unless she did so, someone or other of Richard's cousins would be heir to the crown. I have spoken of his cousin Henry of Bolingbroke as the principal of these claimants. There was, however, another one, Roger, the Earl of March. Roger was the grandson of Richard's uncle Lionel, who had died long before. The Duke of Gloucester, who had been so bitterly opposed to Richard's marriage with Isabella, and had, as it seemed, now become his implacable enemy, conceived the plan of deposing Richard and making Roger king. Isabella, if this plan had been carried into effect, was to have been shut up in a prison for all the rest of her days. There were several great nobles joined with the Duke of Gloucester in this conspiracy.

The plot was betrayed to Richard by some of the confederates. Richard immediately determined to arrest his uncle and bring him to trial. It was necessary, however, to do this secretly, before any of the conspirators should be put upon their guard. So he set off one night from his palace in Westminster, with a considerable company of armed men, to go to the duke's palace, which was at some distance from London, planning his journey so as to arrive there very early in the morning. The people of London, when they saw the king passing at that late hour, wondered where he was going.

He arrived very early the next morning at the duke's castle. He sent some of his men forward into the court of the castle to ask if the duke were at home. The servants said that he was at home, but he was not yet up. So the messengers sent up to him in his bedchamber to inform him that the king was below, and to ask him to come down and receive him. Gloucester accordingly came down. He was much surprised, but he knew that it would be very unwise for him to show any suspicion, and so, after welcoming the king, he asked what was the object of so early a visit. The king assumed a gay and unconcerned air, as if he were out upon some party of pleasure, and said he wished the duke to go away with him a short distance. So the duke dressed himself and mounted his horse, the king, in the meantime, talking in a merry way with the ladies of the castle who had come down into the court to receive him. When they were ready the whole party rode out of the court, and then the king, suddenly changing his tone, ordered his men to arrest the duke and take him away.

The duke was never again seen or heard of in England, and for a long time it was not known what had become of him. It was, however, at last said, and generally believed, that he was put on board a ship, and sent secretly to Calais, and shut up in a castle there, and was, after a time, strangled by means of feather beds, or, as others say, by wet towels put over his face, in obedience to orders sent to the castle by Richard. Several other great noblemen, whom Richard supposed to be confederates with Gloucester, were arrested by similar stratagems. Two or three of the most powerful of them were brought to a trial before judges in Richard's interest, and, being condemned, were beheaded. It is supposed that Richard did not dare to bring Gloucester himself to trial, on account of the great popularity and vast influence which he enjoyed among the people of England.

Richard was very much pleased with the success of his measures for thus putting the most formidable of his enemies out of the way, and not long after this his cousin Roger died, so that Richard was henceforth relieved of all special apprehension on his account. But the country was extremely dissatisfied. The Duke of Gloucester had been very much respected and beloved by the nation. Richard was hated. His government was tyrannical. His style of living was so extravagant that his expenses were enormous, and the people were taxed beyond endurance to raise the money required. While, however, he thus spared no expense to secure his own personal aggrandizement and glory, it was generally believed that he cared little for the substantial interests of the country, but was ready to sacrifice them at any time to promote his own selfish ends.

In the meantime, having killed the principal leaders opposed to him, for a time he had everything his own way. He obtained the control of Parliament, and caused the most unjust and iniquitous laws to be passed, the object of which was to supply him more and more fully with money, and to increase still more his own personal power. He went on in this way until the country was almost ripe for rebellion.

Still, with all his wealth and splendor, Richard was not happy. He was harassed by perpetual suspicions and anxieties, and his conscience tortured him with reproaches for the executions which he had procured of his uncle Gloucester and the other noblemen, particularly the Earl of Arundel, one of the most powerful and wealthy nobles of England. He used to awake from his sleep at night in horror, crying out that the blood of the earl was all over his bed.

He was afraid continually of his cousin Henry, who was now in the direct line of succession to the crown, and whom he imagined to be conspiring against him. He wished very much to find some means of removing him out of the way. An opportunity at length presented itself. There was a quarrel between Henry and a certain nobleman named Norfolk. Each accused the other of treasonable designs. There was a long difficulty about it, and several plans were formed for a trial of the case. At last it was determined that there should be a trial by single combat between the parties, to determine the question which of them was the true man.

The town of Coventry, which is in the central part of England, was appointed for this combat. The lists were prepared, a pavilion for the use of the king and those who were to act as judges was erected, and an immense concourse of spectators assembled to witness the contest. All the preliminary ceremonies were performed, as usual in those days in personal combats of this character, except that in this case the combatants were to fight on horseback. They came into the lists with horses magnificently caparisoned. Norfolk's horse was covered with crimson velvet, and the trappings of Henry's were equally splendid. When all was ready, the signal was given, and the battle commenced. After the combatants had made a few passes at each other without effect, the king made a signal, and the heralds cried out, Ho! Ho! which was an order for them to stop. The king then directed that their arms should be taken from them, and that they should dismount, and take their places in certain chairs which had been provided for them within the lists. These chairs were very gorgeous in style and workmanship, being covered with velvet, and elegantly embroidered.

The assembly waited a long time while the king and those with him held a consultation. At length the king announced that the combat was to proceed no farther, but that both parties were deemed guilty, and that they were both to be banished from the realm. The term of Henry's banishment was ten years; Norfolk's was for life.

The country was greatly incensed at this decision. There was no proof whatever that Henry had done anything wrong. Henry, however, submitted to the king's decree, apparently without murmuring, and took his departure. As he journeyed toward Dover, where he was to embark, the people flocked around him at all the towns and villages that he passed through, and mourned his departure; and when finally he embarked at Dover and went away, they said that the only shield, defense, and comfort of the commonwealth was gone.

Henry went to Paris, and there told his story to the King of France. The king took his part very decidedly. He received him in a very cordial and friendly manner, and condemned the course which Richard had pursued.

Another circumstance occurred to alienate the King of France still more from Richard. There was a certain French lady, named De Courcy, who had come from France with the little queen, and had since occupied a high position in the queen's household. She was Isabella's governess and principal lady of honor. This lady, it seemed, lived in quite an expensive style, and by her influence and management greatly increased the expense of the queen's establishment, which was, of course, entirely independent of that of the king. This Lady De Courcy kept eighteen horses for her own personal use, and maintained a large train of attendants to accompany her in state whenever she appeared in public. She had two or three goldsmiths and jewelers, and two or three furriers, and a proportionate number of other artisans all the time at work, making her dresses and decorations. Richard, under pretense that he could not afford all this, dismissed the Lady De Courcy from her office, and sent her home to France. Of course she was very indignant at this treatment, and she set out on her return home, prepared to give the King of France a very unfavorable account of his son-in-law. It was some time after this, however, before she arrived at Paris.

About three months after Henry of Bolingbroke was banished from the realm, his father, the Duke of Lancaster, died. He left immense estates, which of right should have descended to his son. Richard had given Henry leave to appoint an attorney to act as his agent during his banishment, and take care of his property; but, instead of allowing this attorney to take possession of these estates, and hold them for Henry until he should return, the king confiscated them, and seized them himself. He also, at the same time, revoked the powers which he had granted to the attorney. This transaction awakened one general burst of indignation from one end of England to the other, and greatly increased the hatred which the people bore to the king, and the favor with which they were disposed to regard Henry.

It must be admitted, in justice to Richard, that his mind was greatly harassed at this time with the troubles and difficulties that surrounded him, and with his want of money. To complete his misfortunes, a rebellion broke out in Ireland. He felt compelled to go himself and quell it. So he collected all the money that he could obtain, and raised an army and equipped a fleet to go across the Irish Sea. He left his uncle, the Duke of York, regent during his absence.

Before setting out for Ireland, the king went to Windsor to bid the little queen good-by. He took his leave of her in a church at Windsor, where she accompanied him to mass. On leaving the church after service, he partook of wine and refreshments with her at the door, and then lifting her up in his arms, he kissed her many times, saying,

"Adieu, madame. Adieu till we meet again."

As soon as Richard was gone, a great number of the leading and influential people began to form plans to keep him from coming back again, or at least to prevent his ever again ruling over the realm. Henry, who was now in Paris, and who, since his father was dead, was now himself the Duke of Lancaster, began to receive letters from many persons urging him to come to England, and promising him their support in dispossessing Richard of the throne.

Henry determined at length to comply with these proposals. He found many persons in France to encourage him, and some to join him. With these persons, not more, it is said, than sixty in all, he set sail from the coast of France, and, passing across the Channel, approached the coast of England. He touched at several places, to ascertain what was the feeling of the country toward him. At length he was encouraged to land. The people received him joyfully, and every body flocked to his standard.

The Duke of York, whom Richard had left as regent, immediately called a council of Richard's friends to consider what it was best to do. On consultation and inquiry, they found that the country would not support them in any plan for resisting Henry. So they abandoned Richard's cause at once in despair, and fled in various directions, intent only on saving their own lives.

The Duke of York went to Windsor Castle, took the queen and her attendants, and conveyed them up the river to the Castle of Wallingford, where he thought they would be more safe.

In the meantime, the king's expedition to Ireland resulted disastrously, and he returned to England. To his utter dismay, he learned, on his arrival, that Henry had landed in England, and was advancing toward London in a triumphant manner. He had no sufficient force under his command to enable him to go and meet his cousin with any hope of success. The only question was how he could save himself from Henry's vengeance. He dismissed the troops that remained with him, and then, with a very few attendants to accompany him, he sought refuge for a while among the castles in Wales, where he was reduced to great destitution and distress, being forced sometimes to sleep on straw. At length he went to Conway, which is a town near the northern confines of Wales, and shut himself up in the castle there—that famous Conway Castle, the ruins of which are so much visited and admired by the tourists of the present day.

In the meantime, Henry, although he had marched triumphantly through England at the head of a large, though irregular force, had not proclaimed himself king, or taken any other open step inconsistent with his allegiance to Richard. But now, when he heard that Richard was in Wales, he went thither himself at the head of quite a large army which he had raised in London. He stopped at a town in North Wales called Flint, and, taking his lodgings there, he sent forward an earl as his messenger to Conway Castle to treat with Richard. The earl, on being introduced into Richard's presence, said that his cousin was at Flint Castle, and wished that he would come there to confer with him on matters of great moment. Richard did not know what to do. He soon reflected, however, that he was completely in Henry's power, and that he might as well make a virtue of necessity, and submit with a good grace; so he said he would accompany the earl to Flint Castle.

They had not gone far on the road before a large number of armed men appeared at the road side, in a narrow place between the mountains and the sea, where they had been lying in ambush. These men were under the earl's command. Little was said, but Richard saw that he was a prisoner.

On his arrival at Flint Castle, Richard had an interview with Henry. Henry, when he came into the king's presence, treated him with all due reverence, as if he still acknowledged him as his sovereign. He kneeled repeatedly as he advanced, until at length the king took him by the hand and raised him up, saying, at the same time,

"Dear cousin, you are welcome."

Henry replied,

"My sovereign lord and king, the cause of my coming at this time is to have again the restitution of my person, my lands, and my heritage, through your majesty's gracious permission."

The king replied,

"Dear cousin, I am ready to accomplish your will, so that you may enjoy all that is yours without exception."

After some farther insincere and hypocritical conversation of this sort, breakfast was served. After breakfast, Henry conducted the king to a window on the wall, from which, on looking over the plain, a vast number of armed men, who had come from London with Henry, were to be seen. Richard asked who those men were. Henry replied that they were people of London.

"And what do they want?" asked Richard.

"They want me to take *you*," said Henry, "and carry you prisoner to the Tower; and there will be no pacifying them unless you go with me."

Richard saw at once that it was useless to make any resistance, so he submitted himself entirely to such arrangements as Henry might make. Henry accordingly set out with him on the journey to London, ostensibly escorting him as a king, but really conveying him as a prisoner. On the journey, the fallen monarch suffered many marks of neglect and indignity, but he knew that he was wholly in the power of his enemies, and that it was useless to complain; indeed, his spirit was completely broken, and he had no heart to make even a struggle. On reaching London, he was conducted to the Tower. He was lodged there as he had often been lodged before, only now the guards which surrounded him were under the command of his enemies, and were placed there to prevent his escape, instead of to protect him from danger.

Henry immediately convened a Parliament, issuing the writs, however, in the king's name. This was necessary, to make the Parliament technically legal. When the Parliament met, articles of accusation were formally brought against Richard. These articles were thirty-three in number. They recapitulated all the political crimes and offenses which Richard had committed during his life, his cruelties and oppressions, his wastefulness, his maladministration of public affairs, the illegal and unjust sentences of banishment or of death which he had pronounced upon peers of the realm, and various other high crimes and misdemeanors.

While these measures were pending, Richard's mind was in a state of dreadful suspense and agitation. Sometimes he sank into the greatest depths of despondency and gloom, and sometimes he raved like a madman, walking to and fro in his apartment in his phrensy, vowing vengeance on his enemies.

He had interviews from time to time with Henry and the other nobles. At one time Henry went with the Duke of York and others to the Tower, and sent a messenger to the king, requesting him to come to the apartment where they were, as they wished to see him.

"Tell Henry of Lancaster," said the king, "that I shall do no such thing. If he wishes to see me, let him come to me."

So they came to the king's apartment. Henry took off his cap as he came in, and saluted the king respectfully. The Duke of York was with Henry at this time. Richard was very angry with the Duke of York, whom he had left regent of England when he went away, but who had made no resistance to Henry's invasion. So, as soon as he saw him, he broke forth in a perfect phrensy of vituperation and rage against him, and against his son, who was also present. This produced a violent altercation between them and the king, in which one of them told the king that he lied, and threw down his bonnet before him in token of defiance. Richard then turned to Henry, and demanded, in a voice of fury, why he was placed thus in confinement, under a guard of armed men.

"Am I your servant," he demanded, "or am I your king? And what do you intend to do with me?"

"You are my king and lord," replied Henry, calmly, "but the Parliament have determined that you are to be kept in confinement for the present, until they can decide in respect to the charges laid against you."

Here the king uttered a dreadful imprecation, expressive of rage and despair.

He then demanded that they should let him have his wife. But Henry replied that the council had forbidden that he should see the queen. This exasperated the king more than ever. He walked to and fro across the apartment, wringing his hands, and uttering wild and incoherent expressions of helpless rage.

The end of it was that Richard was forced to abdicate the crown. He soon saw that it was only by so doing that he could hope to save his life. An assembly was convened, and he formally delivered up his crown, and renounced all claim to it forever. He also gave up the globe and sceptre, the emblems of sovereignty, with which he had been invested at his coronation. In addition to this ceremony, a written deed of abdication had been drawn up, and this deed was now signed by the king with all the necessary formalities. Proclamation having been made of Richard's abdication, Henry came forward and claimed the crown as Richard's rightful successor, and he was at once proclaimed king, and conducted to the throne. Richard was conducted back to the Tower, and soon afterward was conveyed, by Henry's order, to a more sure place of confinement—Pontefract Castle, and here was shut up a close prisoner.

Henry Of Bolingbroke—King Henry IV

Things remained in this state a short time, and then a rumor arose that a conspiracy was formed by Richard's friends to murder Henry, and restore Richard to the throne. A spiked instrument was said to have been found in Henry's bed, put there by some of the conspirators, with a view of destroying him when he lay down. Whether this story of the conspiracy was false or true, one thing is certain, that the existence of Richard endangered greatly the continuance and security of Henry's power. Henry and his counselors were well aware of this; and one day, when they had been conversing on the subject of this danger, Henry said, "Have I no faithful friend who will deliver me from this man, whose life is death to me, and whose death would be my life?"

Pontefract Castle, King Richard's Prison

Very soon after this, it was known that Richard was dead. The universal belief was that he was murdered. There were various rumors in respect to the manner in which the deed was perpetrated. The account most precise and positive states that a man named Exton, who had heard the remark of the king, repaired at once to the castle of Pontefract, accompanied by eight desperate men, all well-armed, and gained admission to Richard's room while he was at table. Richard, seeing his danger, sprang up, and attempted to defend himself. He wrenched a weapon out of the hands of one of his assailants, and fought with it so furiously that he cut down four of the ruffians before he was overpowered. He was felled to the floor at last by a blow which Exton struck him upon his head, Exton having sprung up upon the chair which Richard had sat in, and thus obtained an advantage by his high position.

It was necessary to make the fact of Richard's death very certain, and so, soon afterward, the body was placed upon a hearse, and drawn by four black horses to London. Here it was left in a public place for some time, to be viewed by all who desired to view it. There were no less than *twenty thousand* persons that availed themselves of the opportunity of satisfying themselves, by the evidence of their senses, that the hated Richard was no more.

* * *

The little queen all this time had been confined in another castle. She was now about twelve years old. Her father, when he heard of the misfortunes which had befallen her husband, and of the forlorn and helpless condition in which she was placed, was so distressed that he became insane. The other members of the family sent to England to demand that she should be restored to them, but Henry refused this request. He wished to make her the wife of his son, who was now the Prince of Wales, but Isabella would not listen to any such proposals. Then Henry wished that she should remain in England as the queen-dowager, and he promised that she should be treated with the greatest respect and consideration as long as she lived; but neither she herself nor her friends in France would consent to this. At length, after long delay, and many protracted negotiations, it was decided that she should return home.

The little queen, on her return to France, embarked from Dover. There were five vessels appointed to receive her and her suite. There were in attendance upon her two ladies of the royal family, who had the charge of her person, her governess, several maids of honor, and two French chambermaids, whose names were Semonette and Marianne. There were many other persons besides.

Isabella reached the French frontier at a town between Calais and Boulogne, and there was delivered, with much form and ceremony, to a deputation of French authorities sent forward to receive her.

She lived in France after this for several years, mourning her husband all the time with faithful and unchanging affection. At length a marriage was arranged for her with her cousin, a French prince. She was married when she was nineteen years old. She was very averse to this marriage when it was first proposed to her, and could only speak of it with tears; but, under all the circumstances of the case, she thought that she was not at liberty to decline it, and after she was married she loved her husband very sincerely, and made a very devoted and faithful wife. Three years after her marriage she had a son, and a few hours after the birth of the child she suddenly died. Her husband was almost distracted when he heard that his beloved wife was dead. His grief seemed, for a time, perfectly uncontrollable; but when they brought to him his infant child, it seemed in some measure to comfort him.

THE END

ABOUT JACOB ABBOTT

Jacob Abbott was born in Hallowell, Maine in 1803, the son of a minister and farmer. Even as a young boy, he showed academic promise and an interest in spiritual matters. After attending the Hallowell Academy, he was admitted to Bowdoin College at the age of 14.

At Bowdoin, Abbott studied classics and mathematics. He graduated second in his class in 1820 at the young age of 16. He was known as a serious and studious young man who strove for excellence.

After college, Abbott went on to study at Andover Theological Seminary with the intention of becoming a Congregationalist minister. However, his rigorous study habits and frail health caused him to abandon this pursuit after just two years.

Abbott was plagued by gastrointestinal issues and migraines throughout his life, likely exacerbated by the demanding academic environment. His poor health finally forced him to leave his ministerial studies and turn to the less stressful pursuits of writing and tutoring.

First, Abbott took a job as a professor of mathematics and natural philosophy at Amherst College in 1824. The following year, he married Harriet Vaughan and moved to Boston where he opened a school for young ladies. It was during this time that he began writing simple textbooks for teaching science, history and Christian values.

So while Abbott had aspired to be a minister, chronic health issues led him to find an alternate calling educating children through clear and engaging writing. This pivot would launch his successful career as one of the most famous children's authors of the 19th century.

In 1825, Abbott married Harriet Vaughan and soon after started his own school for young ladies in Boston. During this time, he began

ABOUT JACOB ABBOTT

writing educational books in a popular, simple style. His early works included the Mount Vernon Reader and The Young Christian.

Abbott gained fame with the Rollo series, first published in 1835. These stories followed a young boy named Rollo learning morals and virtues through his everyday adventures. The series was hugely popular and established Abbott's reputation as a gifted children's writer.

Other notable books by Abbott include the Franconia Stories (1853-1873), a 10-volume series about a brother and sister's adventures in the country, and the Marco Paul series (1853-1873), which followed a boy's travels around America learning about each state.

In all, Jacob Abbott wrote over 200 books, primarily for young readers. His works were praised for their ability to educate and impart moral lessons in an engaging, story-driven way. Though largely forgotten today, he was one of the most prolific and beloved children's authors of his era.

Abbott continued writing up until his death on October 31, 1879 in Farmington, Maine. His legacy lives on through his contributions to 19th century children's literature.

BIOGRAPHIES ABBOTT WROTE

A number of the books Abbott wrote were biographies of famous people. Famous characters covered in these books included:

Alexander the Great: This book provides a sweeping look at the life and achievements of Alexander III of Macedon, better known as Alexander the Great. It follows his early education by Aristotle, ascension to the throne after his father Philip II's assassination, and extensive military campaigns across Asia and northeast Africa. Abbott recounts Alexander's major battles against the Persians and annexation of their empire. The book also examines Alexander's tactics, military innovations, and creation of a Hellenistic empire stretching from Greece to India before his death at 32.

Alfred the Great: This biography focuses on Alfred's defense of the Kingdom of Wessex against Viking raids in 9th century England. It discusses how Alfred drove back the Great Heathen Army and then negotiated terms with the Vikings, designating parts of England for their settlement. Abbott also highlights Alfred's efforts to revive learning and education in England, as well as his codification of laws and strengthening of the Anglo-Saxon navy. The book frames Alfred as a scholarly, strategic and devout ruler whose achievements laid the foundation for a unified England.

King Charles I: This book looks at the reign of Charles I leading up to and during the English Civil War. It focuses on the religious and political conflicts between Charles I and Parliament, caused largely by

Charles' belief in divine right of kings and many unpopular, authoritarian policies. Abbott also examines Charles' refusal to compromise, leading to the war against Parliament's New Model Army and his eventual execution for treason in 1649 under Oliver Cromwell.

King Charles II: This biography deals with the restoration of the English monarchy under Charles II after the death of Oliver Cromwell. It follows Charles II's return from exile and re-establishment of royal power. However, Abbott also notes Charles' own conflicts with Parliament and religious controversies during his reign. The book discusses Charles' hedonistic lifestyle and many mistresses, but also his support for science, exploration and trade that helped expand the British Empire.

Cleopatra: This book examines Cleopatra VII's life and rule over ancient Egypt. Abbott chronicles Cleopatra's relationships and political alliances with Julius Caesar and Mark Antony, as she sought to maintain Egypt's independence from Rome. The biography highlights Cleopatra's intelligence, education and strategic skills in dealing with Rome. But it ultimately focuses on Cleopatra's downfall and suicide after Mark Antony's defeat by Octavian, leading to Egypt becoming a Roman province.

Cyrus the Great: This biography covers Cyrus II of Persia, founder of the Achaemenid Empire. Abbott traces Cyrus's rise from Persian prince, to revolt against the Medes, to conqueror of the Lydian and Babylonian empires. The book also examines Cyrus's leadership qualities and tolerant policies toward conquered peoples. It portrays Cyrus as a wise, inspirational leader who created the model of a centralized Persian state.

Darius: This book looks at the reign of Darius I, examining his consolidation of the Persian Empire through administrative reforms, development of infrastructure, and expansion of territory. Abbott discusses

Darius's división of the empire into provinces and implementation of a uniform tax system and coinage. The biography also covers his invasion of Greece which was thwarted at the famous Battle of Marathon. Overall, it presents Darius as an capable, pragmatic ruler under whom the Persian Empire reached its zenith.

Queen Elizabeth: This biography celebrates the long and prosperous reign of Queen Elizabeth I of England. Abbott focuses on Elizabeth's shrewd leadership, religious compromise, and patronage of the arts and literature that fostered English Renaissance culture. The book also highlights Elizabeth's naval defeat of the Spanish Armada which secured England's independence from Europe. Overall, Abbott portrays Elizabeth as a commanding, canny and popular female ruler who strengthened England as a major world power.

Genghis Khan: This book looks at the incredible rise of Temüjin, better known as Genghis Khan. It follows his hardships as an outcast youth to becoming the fearsome founder of the Mongol Empire. Abbott chronicles Genghis Khan's brilliant military tactics and utterly ruthless conquests that allowed the Mongols to dominate much of Asia and Eastern Europe. Overall it paints him as a complex figure--strategic genius but also brutal tyrant.

Hannibal: This biography focuses on the great Carthaginian general Hannibal Barca. It recounts his famous crossing of the Alps with war elephants and invasion of Italy during the Second Punic War against Rome. Abbott details Hannibal's victories in major battles like Cannae but also his eventual defeat by Scipio and exile. The book celebrates Hannibal's daring military prowess but also concession late in life that Rome could not be conquered.

Josephine: This book examines the life of Josephine Bonaparte from her aristocratic upbringing in Martinique to her marriage to Napoleon Bonaparte. It focuses on Josephine's time as Empress consort of France and her support for arts and education. But it also discusses Napoleon's eventual divorce from her due to dynastic pressures. Overall the book presents Josephine as an intelligent, compassionate woman who tempered some of Napoleon's ambition.

Julius Caesar: This traces Caesar's life from early military campaigns to dictator and eventual assassination. Abbott covers Caesar's conquest of Gaul, rivalry with Pompey, famously crossing the Rubicon and crowning as dictator. The biography also examines the conspiracy led by Brutus and Cassius to assassinate Caesar in order to save the Roman Republic. In all, the book presents Caesar as an unmatched military mind who irrevocably changed the Roman Empire.

Margaret of Anjou: This biography looks at Margaret of Anjou who became queen consort to England's King Henry VI. It focuses on the political intrigue and machinations Margaret became involved in to support her husband's reign during the War of the Roses. Abbott portrays Margaret as a fiercely devoted, cunning woman who backed the Lancastrians against factions like the Yorkists led by Richard Neville. Though she lost power, the book frames her as a dominant figure during the conflict.

Mary, Queen of Scots: This book examines the life of Mary Stuart who became Queen of Scotland as an infant. It follows her tumultuous reign marked by scandals and plots to overthrow her by Protestants. Her Catholicism also put her at odds with England's Elizabeth I. Abbott recounts Mary's forced abdication, escape to England, and eventual execution ordered by Elizabeth for plotting against her. Overall it presents a tragic figure whose life was marked by political and religious turmoil.

Nero: This biography looks at the notorious Roman emperor Nero. It explores his self-indulgent lifestyle and tyrannical rule marked by possible matricide and the brutal execution of Christians. Abbott also examines legends around Nero like his fiddling during the Great Fire of Rome. The book presents a despotic, unstable man who drastically weakened the Roman Empire.

Peter the Great: This book covers the reforms and policies of Peter the Great that rapidly westernized Russia. Abbott discusses Peter's extensive European travels as a youth and later programs to remake Russia's army, expand its naval fleet, and build a new capital in St. Petersburg. The biography also examines Peter's harsh, authoritarian approach to governing that consolidated his power. Overall it presents him as a pivotal, transformative tsar.

Pyrrhus: This examines the life and military exploits of Pyrrhus, king of Epirus. It focuses on his campaigns against Rome where he won major battles but suffered heavy losses, giving rise to the term "Pyrrhic victory." Abbott recounts Pyrrhus's struggles to build a Greek empire and failed invasion of Sicily against Carthage. Though a skilled commander, Pyrrhus ultimately failed to achieve lasting gains.

Richard I: This biography looks at the reign of Richard I, known as Lionheart. It focuses on Richard's leadership during the Third Crusade to recapture Jerusalem from Saladin. Abbott also details the legendary tales of Richard's bravery and valor in campaigns against France and during his imprisonment. Overall, the book presents Richard I as one of England's great warrior kings.

Richard II: This explores the reign and overthrow of King Richard II. Abbott covers Richard's despotic actions that led the nobles to revolt and install Henry IV, leading to Richard's imprisonment and likely murder. The biography presents a weak king whose tyranny and poor leadership during a peasant's revolt cost him power and his life.

Richard III: This delves into the controversial rule of Richard III. Abbott examines Richard's contested path to the throne and the disappearance of the Princes in the Tower which Richard likely ordered. It also portrays Richard's defeat at the hands of Henry Tudor at the Battle of Bosworth Field that ended the Wars of the Roses. Ultimately Abbott paints Richard III as willing to employ any means to gain and retain the English crown.

Romulus: This recounts the Roman legend of Romulus and Remus, twin brothers raised by a she-wolf who went on to found the city of Rome. Abbott covers the myths of the brothers' quarrel over leadership, with Romulus killing Remus and becoming Rome's first king and architect of its nascent political institutions. Though mythological, Romulus represents ancient Rome's founding origins and rise to power.

William the Conqueror: This biography follows William, Duke of Normandy's conquest of England in 1066 after victory at the Battle of Hastings. Abbott discusses William's reign as king where he consolidated control, introduced feudalism, and fused English and Norman culture. William is presented as a formidable, innovative Norman leader who irrevocably transformed Anglo-Saxon England.

Xerxes: This examines the reign of Xerxes I of Persia, known for his failed invasion of Greece. Abbott focuses on Xerxes's gathering of a massive army to crush Greek resistance, but defeat at Salamis ended his ambitions. The book covers later unrest and palace intrigue that clouded the end of Xerxes's reign. Overall he is portrayed as a rash ruler whose desire for conquest led to disaster for Persia.

www.ingramcontent.com/pod-product-compliance
Lightning Source LLC
Chambersburg PA
CBHW070056080526
44586CB00013B/1078